GOLD ALWAYS WINS

GOLD ALWAYS WINS

How the Yellow Metal Defies its Critics

ROBIN BROMBY

Highgate

HIGHGATE PUBLISHING - SYDNEY

GOLD ALWAYS WINS: How the yellow metal defies its critics

ISBN 978-0-9925956-2-3

First published in 2015 by Highgate Publishing

This revised and expanded edition published 2018

Highgate Publishing,

P O Box 481,

Edgecliff NSW 2027, Australia.   E: info@highgatepublishing.com.au

CONTENTS

Introduction..1

1. How the Critics got it Wrong...............................13

2. What history teaches us about gold.....................31

3. Gold is money..45

4. It's all about the fundamentals............................53

5. Gold booms and busts..65

6. How Hard is it to Find Gold................................67

Postscript...73

Appendix 1: Gold as a Financial Instrument...........77

Appendix 2: Silver, the Poor Relation....................81

Appendix 3: Gold Facts...93

All metal prices are in US dollars unless otherwise stated.

There is a great misunderstanding of what the noted economist John Maynard Keynes said. He never said that gold was
itself a barbarous relic.
His actual words:

"In truth, the gold <u>standard</u> is already a barbarous relic"

... which, I think you would agree, is quite a different matter!

INTRODUCTION

BACK IN 1930, *TIME* magazine was really worried about gold — or, at least, the newsmagazine reported that bankers and economists were. 'Australian gold fields are almost exhausted. U. S. production has fallen steadily (from $101,000,000 in 1915 to $45,000,000 in 1928),' it reported. But while bankers and economists were worried, 'metallurgists agree that the discovery of extensive new gold deposits … is unlikely'.

Well, that would not be the first time the 'experts' got it wrong about the yellow metal, would it? Sure, since 1930 there have never again been gold rushes like those of the nineteenth century in California, New Zealand, the Yukon and the Australian state of Victoria, but since 1930 quite a lot of gold has been found; just think of West Africa and the huge deposits identified along the Birimian Greenstone Belt.

And what about that declining gold supply? In 1915, the year mentioned above, world gold production was 585 tonnes. In 2014, the world's mines produced 3,133 tonnes, and that represented the sixth successive year of rising output of the metal. Mind you, the gold market in total (that means gold trading of both physical gold and gold derivatives) is many times larger than the amount of physical gold that is poured each year by mining companies and then refined. The London Bullion Market Association members in 2014 traded 157,000 tonnes of gold. When you con-

1

sider that it is estimated by London-based Thomson Reuters GFMS that 183,000 tonnes of gold has been mined in human history, that gives you some idea of the trading in a metal that is always being written off. In fact, if you take the entire world derivatives plus physical trade, that amounts to $22 trillion a year — or 188 times annual gold mine production.

In 1930, too, the Soviet Union was stepping up gold exploration (and would use Gulag prisoners to mine much of it). Tsarist Russia had been big into gold mining but, after the 1917 Communist revolution, the precious metal was initially considered just another manifestation of detested capitalism. Indeed, in 1921 Lenin proclaimed: 'When we are victorious on a world-wide scale we will make public toilets out of gold on the streets of the world's largest cities'. He was not proposing the equivalent of burning $100 bills as a demonstration of wealth destruction; no, Lenin thought gold would become worthless and there would be no better use for it than giving a bit of glint and gleam to public conveniences. According to Nikita Khrushchev's memoirs, Lenin had argued that, at a certain stage of human society's development, gold would lose its value. In the meantime, Lenin said to keep the gold; when full communism had been established, gold would no longer be a means of exchange and the metal could be used to decorate public toilets.

It took just six years for that attitude to go out the window in the Union of Socialist Soviet Republics. By 1927 Joseph Stalin was pushing expansion of gold mining in order to pay for imports needed for his industrialization program, and to help pay off Soviet debts. A slump in soft commodities meant Russian export income from timber and grain had collapsed. And, by 1943, *The Economist* was quoting a leading Soviet government figure, Alexander Serebrovsky, arguing for a return to the gold standard — by which time, the magazine reported, the U.S.S.R was the second largest gold producer in the world. (Serebrovsky would four years later fall a victim of the purges, being shot on the trumped up charge of sending gold bars to Leon Trotsky, Stalin's arch-enemy.)

Indeed, in 1934 Serebrovsky, who had been charged by Stalin with the task of reviving gold production, vowed that the U.S.S.R would soon overtake the Transvaal as a producer, making it the largest in the world

Gold: written off nearly 100 years ago, still demeaned by the anti-gold crowd today. They never learn.

And here is another little slice of history pertinent at a time when China is the world's leading gold producer (and consumer). At one stage it was widely believed China did not possess any great mineral wealth. In 1872 the then eminent geologist, Baron Ferdinand von Richthofen (incidentally, he was the uncle of the 'Red Baron' World War I flying ace, Manfred von Richthofen) who had made several trips to China, told the Shanghai Chamber of Commerce: 'The great number of places in which gold is washed from the river sand in China, far from furnishing proof of the wealth of the country, is clear evidence of the superabundance of human labour, prevalence of low wages, and the poverty of the individuals engaged in the search'.

⊖⸜⸝⸜⸝⸜⸝⊖

Why do we pay so much attention to what analysts have to say about gold? I have not kept count, but all the way through the 2001 to 2011 gold bull market you could always find some market watchers predicting imminent doom for the yellow metal. Much of the commentary in the mainstream media when it comes to gold is vapid, ill informed and, well, dopey.

Don't agree? Then read these items from just one week back in July 2011:

* **Tuesday's news:** 'Money managers have slashed their net long, or bullish, positioning in U.S. gold futures and options to the lowest level in more than four months and in silver to the lowest level in more than a year, according to the most recent data from the Commodity Futures Trading Commission.'

* **Wednesday's news:** 'Gold rallied strongly on debt concerns, says HSBC. The bank cites a Standard & Poor's announcement that it may lower its rating on Greece to selective default if a plan by banks to roll over Greek debt holdings is implemented. Also, gold benefited from a Moody's warning that China may have understated local government debt, as well as the U.S. deficit-ceiling impasse.' (That was the night that gold rose $30/oz.)

* **Thursday's news:** 'Gold futures closed at their highest level in two weeks Wednesday, with global debt troubles helping it tally a two-session win of nearly $47 an ounce'.

So, what would it be tomorrow, I asked at the time? If gold's price went down, then I warned that readers could expect news reports the following morning to say something along the lines of 'investors sold gold as fears of European default eased' — or whatever the crisis *de jour* may be. Investors, financial commentators, analysts — very few of them show any depth of understanding when it comes to gold. Back in 2011 one yearned to read a news report that said gold had risen/fallen by whatever amount, but that 'this has to be seen against what is an impressive trend over ten years of an accumulating gold price and now the emergence of net central bank buying, not to mention China seemingly trying to corner the gold market', or something like that? One longs today for more insightful treatment of gold in the mainstream media.

All the doubters were voicing their bearish opinions when the figures were showing something else. Take the World Gold Council's table of coin and bar demand. In 2001, it was $3.1 billion (or 357 tonnes); by 2005 it was at $5.6 billion a year (or 393 tonnes). For 2008, demand ended up at $24.1 billion (or 860 tonnes), then fell slightly in 2009 (after the global financial crisis had subsided) both in terms of tonnage and value and then in 2010 hit an astonishing $39 billion with demand at 995 tonnes. A tenfold increase in ten years in dollar terms; but that trend did little to discourage the gold bears.

Between 1988 (in the aftermath of the 1987 stock market crash) and 2007, I was following the gold story at close quarters, being a reporter on *The Australian* newspaper, and based in Sydney. I followed the junior gold stocks through the terrible 1990s, during which the gold price bounced along the bottom and exploration began to shrivel. The small explorers, the companies on which the industry depends to drill away and find deposits large and small, were hamstrung by their inability to raise fresh finance. So many of these companies fled the mining sector and sought survival in technology as the dot-com bubble inflated unsustainably. Then I charted the first signs of market ignition in 2002; it was about that gold's rise (and rise and rise) began and would continue through the next decade. I left the newspaper in 2007 but stayed on as a contributor with a weekly column on mining stocks — and kept tags on the gold ones, in particular, and the gold story in general. When the metal retreated in 2013, I was not panicked; to me, it was all about the fundamentals, and the certainty that gold's day had not gone. Much of this belief was based on what China was doing, or presumed to be doing: that is, accumulating gold.

Now, writing this in 2015, I feel no less certain about gold, but very much in a steady-as-she-goes sort of way.

But here's the thing: I am not a gold bug. If the metal suddenly went to $3,000/oz, no one would be more surprised than me. Likewise, if it went to $700/oz I would be no less astonished. Indeed, I believe that gold's shooting toward $1,900/oz in 2011 was, in fact, an overshoot. It had to correct. The $1,900/oz must come again but it seems unlikely there will be a sudden spike (barring, of course, some sort of global financial firestorm).

This book is an attempt to bring a new view to the gold market. It will argue that gold is in the process of reasserting its status as a currency, and a very reliable one at that. However, reliability presumes some degree of stability. And, hence, the more stable behaviour by gold from late 2014 into 2015 might actually be an encouraging sign. The announcement in late May 2015 that China was establishing a $16 billion gold fund — on top of all those yellow bars generally believed (outside China) to be mounting up in the vaults of the People's Bank of China, and the tonnes of gold being accumulated by private Chinese investors, of which more later — just props up my theory.

Gold, I believe, is moving inexorably to be the ultimate store of value once again. But, unless there is some extraordinary financial implosion (in which case all bets are off) that fulfills the gold bug dream of $3,000, $5,000 or $10,000, it is going to be slow but steady. Gold may even turn out to be the most solid rock in the financial pool.

This is a very complex story, not that you would guess it from the bulk of commentary. So here is my plea: before anyone opens their mouth to make a 'sell' order or hits the computer keys on the subject of gold — pause, and then think. Think about that ten-year winning streak, an extraordinary run for the yellow metal (followed by reasonably stable performance after the initial retreat from its highs). Think about the fact the central banks are now in a net buying position so far as gold is concerned. Think about China importing huge amounts of gold (and the Vietnamese, too). Think about the ongoing uncertainty throughout the world economy? And think about how much debt — government, business, personal — is swirling around the globe in its trillions? And think about derivatives: according to the Bank of International Settlements in 2014, the total positions held equate to about $700 trillion; others believe it may be closer to one quadrillion dollars.

Think about what all those things portend for the appeal of a gold bar under the bed.

No one gets petulant about iron ore, nickel or even molybdenum. But, boy, does gold bring the fighters out of their corners. The gold enthusiasts wring their hands in despair at the blindness of others not being able to see the world is on the brink of disaster and are not, like them, squirrelling away gold bars and coins (and laying in a year's supply of tinned food into the bargain). The sceptics, for their part, don't actually say they believe the gold bugs are a bunch of nut cases, but you know that is what they are thinking.

At a guess, between eighty per cent and ninety per cent of commentary on the gold question is from one of two mutually exclusive positions. One of those is to shrug the shoulders and dismiss gold. You know the argument: holding gold offers no return, the gold bugs have been predicting financial Armageddon since goodness knows when but we're still standing and still operating with paper money, and even the gold stocks' performances have not been all that flash. They say that many of these companies have gone under even while being producers and even many of those that are still with us can't seem to pay regular dividends. All true.

Then there are those who think the sky is about to fall and gold will be the only thing to save them. You get people like the author of one website devoted to the subject of the yellow metal and who posted this: 'I look through hundreds of charts and all the technical analysis and spend most of my free time going to the library looking at economic textbooks and all of the investment audio books. The purpose of all this research is … to profit by finding out how the pattern and the riddle in gold is going to unfold and allow the gold bugs to make massive riches!' The gold websites have long been full to overflowing with frenzied conjecture about the coming collapse of fiat currencies, the end of paper money and — indeed — the end of Civilization as we know it. Possibly. This reporter knows gold bugs and the scale and depth of their obsession (one in particular who has missed out on enormous profits in other metals over the past five years because he could not see past gold).

Surely, there must be middle ground. The problem is that not many want to place themselves on it. Both sides of the gold divide have probably got it wrong. The real story is probably a great deal more prosaic and — dare I say it — somewhere in between the positions taken on opposing sides of the battle lines.

Gold is not the be-all and end-all. But neither is it a thing of the past. It would be worth $3,000 an ounce if the gold bugs were right, $150/oz (or whatever) if those who dismiss gold were on the money. Perhaps we should be thinking of gold in the same light as we view the insurance policy on our houses. You don't mark-to-market that policy on a day-to-day basis, nor do you put every penny you have into insurance. No, insurance is there if the house burns down; gold is there when fiat currencies become more worthless. Likewise, should we be seeing gold as a form of insurance, as a backstop should the world economy go down the drain? This would mean that, like insuring your house, you would spend most of your money elsewhere. But, being prudent, you would have a little physical gold in a safety deposit box and a few gold stocks in the portfolio. After all, there is still real cause for concern about the resilience of the global economy. There are still plenty of people who see what is happening at present as no more than a prolonged sucker rally of the type circa 1931 — a market rebound before the final downward plunge, the rally of the type that deludes most investors and then takes them to ruination.

Fortunately, central bankers around the world have at least tried to avert disaster with bold moves. The fact that they may ultimately fail does not negate the point that no one had any better ideas to try and head off the catastrophe (apart from letting the catastrophe occur and clean out all the bad stuff, a position that has its admirers). But there is a lot that can go wrong, as the global financial crisis demonstrated amply in 2008. So we all need a financial insurance policy. Any better ideas than a ten ounce bar of gold? (And having paid off your mortgage, of course.)

THE CENTRAL BANK STORY

Since the global financial crisis we have seen a dramatic change of heart by the central banks. Who can forget the decisions from the late 1990s by the central banks of Britain, Australia, Switzerland, the Netherlands, Portugal, Spain and France to sell part of their gold holdings (and at the bottom of the market into the bargain with the Swiss alone selling off 1,550 tonnes)? Only the Germans and Italians resisted the temptation (mainly because they were not sure what to do with the proceeds, apparently), which is why they are ranked second (with 3,384.2 tonnes) and fourth (with 2,451.8 tonnes) in terms of central banks holdings of gold (although we all suspect that China has quietly passed both but will drip-feed details to the world, declaring a succession of small amounts over months or years so as to avoid startling the horses by revealing the true position in one hit).

And in mid-2015 we had Austria following the lead of Germany and the Netherlands in deciding they were not comfortable with a large proportion of their gold sitting in foreign vaults and so arranged to have some of the bullion repatriated. Vienna had only seventeen per cent of its 280 tonnes on hand, eighty per cent of the metal held at the Bank of England. Over the next few years, in five tonne loads, much of that was to be moved to Vienna and Switzerland.

Meanwhile, Jordan in 2015 joined the ranks of the central banks to be making the decision to buy more gold, while Kazakhstan added a few more tonnes in March that year to get over the 200 tonne level, more than double where its reserves had stood in 2012.

By that year the trend had become clear, with central banks in 2012 buying 534.6 tonnes. While central bank buying of gold soared, so too was the net cast more widely, with the central banks of Brazil, Paraguay, Iraq and Venezuela topping up their piles of gold bars. But it was also interesting to note that many countries still at that stage had very low proportions of their official reserves in the form of gold. China was the prime example, with only two per cent of its official reserves in gold. Setting aside consideration of drawing equal with the United States (seventy-two per of its official reserves in gold) and passing Germany (sixty-eight per cent), and recognizing that, even if China were aiming for something like Switzerland's 7.7 per cent, that would involve the Chinese central bank buying around 8,116 tonnes, or more than two years' of global mine supply. According to the February 2015 World Gold Council figures, China's then reported 1.054 tonnes of reserves equaled just one per cent of that country's overall official reserves (and the July update made little difference).

Other central banks whose gold holdings, while being in the top forty of holders in tonnage terms, are way below the average are those of Japan (2.4 per cent), Saudi Arabia (1.7 per cent), Thailand (3.8 per cent), Singapore (1.9 per cent) and South Korea (1.1 per cent).

⁕

And, while we're at it, it should be noted that the gold price as expressed in U.S. dollars is gradually losing its influence. As the World Gold Council points out, China and India account for fifty per cent of gold demand and Southeast Asia takes another nine per cent. Today many gold sales are settled in currencies other than the greenback and that trend will continue as more gold exchanges (Thailand wants one) and gold contracts are established in Asia. Which means gold demand will be less and less affected by any surge in the value of the U.S. dollar.

Another point to consider: there is a fundamental flaw in the way gold is valued. That flaw is that market sentiment about the yellow metal is driven largely by the opinions of Western analysts and institutions, among who those positive about gold are in the minority. If they don't actually hate gold, most of the analysts certainly don't like it, they can't figure out why there is so much interest in the metal, and they can't wait to put out client notes predicting the next big fall in the gold price. So here we have gold judged by its value in U.S. dollars and analyzed largely by Western-based analysts.

Meanwhile, in what seems a parallel universe, Asia continues to embrace gold. It is by far the biggest market for the metal and an increasing number of gold transactions take place in currencies other than the U.S. dollar. We have the Shanghai Gold Exchange, while the authorities in Singapore, Malaysia and Thailand all want to get in on the gold trading action.

What other metal impels people to go down to great depths in our oceans to retrieve the sunken treasure? (Indeed, what other metal would justify the description of being 'treasure'? Apart from silver, that is.) The prospect of finding gold and silver has lured many an adventurer. In 2012 *Popular Mechanics* magazine sought expert opinions on how much bullion might still be lying on the seabed around the world. One salvage company said their investigations indicated about $60 billion worth – but that was not adding the historical value of coins, just the value of the contained gold and silver. At that time the Spanish government had gone to court to assert ownership of the galleon *Nuestra Señora de las Mercedes* which had sunk off the Portuguese coast in 1804 with an estimated $500 million worth of coins aboard. In 1988 a salvage company recovered gold bars from the wreck of the *SS*

Central America which had foundered in a storm 320 km off the North Carolina coast in 1857, and was lying 2,200 metres beneath the ocean surface. The ship had been carrying gold from California that was expected by New York banks. Its loss triggered a financial panic in New York. And, more recently, Britain has seen controversy over the supposed four tones of gold that went down with the *HMS Victory* (the predecessor of Nelson's more famous ship of the same name) on its 1744 voyage home from Portugal.

In 2015, as this was being written, a consortium was being formed to salvage bullion from two ships sunk off Ireland in the First World War. The *SS Arabic* was believed to be carrying 1,286,000 ounces of gold being transferred to the American Express and Guaranty Trust in New York City. The vessel, a vessel of the White Star Line (which had also owned *Titanic*) was sunk by U-24. The *RMS Hesperian*, another ship authorized to carry gold and with 482,261 ounces in its holds, was sunk by U-20, the same submarine that had sunk *Lusitania* four months earlier (and part of *Hesperian's* cargo was the casket containing the wife of a Canadian politician who had died during the sinking of that famous passenger liner).

Gold, especially sunken gold, has a lure of it own.

1.

How most Commentators got Gold Wrong

"When the US government stops wasting our resources by trying to maintain the price of gold, its price will sink to . . . $6 an ounce rather than the current $35 an ounce." — Henry Reuss, Chairman of the Joint Economic Committee of Congress, 25 November 1967. *(Needless to say, that did not happen — just one more doom-and-gloom pronouncement that gold proved to be wrong.)*

IN MARCH 2005, THE writing was on the wall. Then the latest figures from the World Gold Council showed that gold availability fell by 13.3 per cent in 2004, the biggest yearly decline in percentage terms since the 1940s, and a product of the severe fall-off in exploration during the malaise years of the 1990s. Mine production was down 4.4 per cent compared with 2003 and totalled 2,478 tonnes. But the overall availability was reduced as producers bought gold to reduce their hedge books and less scrap came on the market. Central bank gold sales also dried up. By 2005 it had been five years since the last greenfield gold discovery in Australia; production from the country's mines in 2004 was 6.5 per cent down on 2003.

And yet, in the face of these facts, so many commentators and analysts continued to bag gold. And gold defied them. And it will continue to defy them again and again.

While we now look back on the period 2002-2011 as a dream run for gold, along the way there were many scary moments when the gold surge seemed to have run out of steam. With each of these pullbacks, there were plenty of commentators only too ready, willing and able to predict the worst.

In June 2007 I was able to note that the metal had taken a sharp dive below $650/oz that month, which gave the gold bears the chance to opine that the boom run was over (six months later gold would finish the year at $834.50/oz). 'We're in one the "gloom" phases, the years of sub-$300 forgotten', I wrote, then added: 'Isn't it time to get a grip?'

At this time Deutsche Bank had just injected A$122 million into an Australian explorer called Crescent Gold for a fifty-five per cent interest. Given the antipathy in the previous twenty years (after the 1987 crash) from the global institutions toward gold, it seemed to me at this time likely that the enormity of the significance of the Deutsche commitment has probably failed to sink in with investors. But what was particularly notable was that too few gold stocks were seeing their share prices rise in anything like parity with the rate of increase in the metal's price. This disconnect between the gold price and the value of gold stocks had puzzled this writer for some time and I knew more than a few gold punters who had been wringing their hands in frustration at this trend.

So it was interesting to see that these concerns had been noted elsewhere. A column in TheStreet.com out of New York in 2007 pondered this very point. That organization had found that the exchange-traded gold fund that it tracked had risen four per cent over the previous six months as the metal price rose but the Amex Gold Bugs index, which tracked a basket of larger precious metals stocks, has dropped five per cent over the same period. Now, TheStreet.com was looking at the big stocks like Newmont Mining and Barrick Gold, with all their cost pressures, labour shortages and the big problem looming over their heads: that is, replacing reserves.

But that did not explain why the majority of Australian gold stocks had performed so badly in the biggest resources boom we had ever seen. One reason for that may have been the view taken by investors: they kept hearing how China had an insatiable appetite for industrial metals — that the country could take all the coal, iron ore, tungsten, zinc, nickel, copper, and so on that other countries could dig out of the ground.

No such anxiety (regarding shortage of supply in the future) existed in relation to gold (and that is still the case). Demand waxes and wanes. All the supply-demand relationships that are of great concern to investors across the commodity range, and which govern market sentiment, were never applied to consideration of gold (not that gold is a commodity, of course — that is one point where I am with the gold bugs). The South African gold industry was by 2007 clearly in decline; Australia had fallen behind in production over the previous few years; there was not too much exploration — anywhere — to speak of in the late 1990s after the metal plunged to $252/oz. And this was at a time when gold prices had been particularly strong considering all that central bank selling.

THE 2008 PANIC

In March 2008 gold finally made it to $1,000/oz. Then, at the end of that month, there was a sharp plunge (it would get worse: by September the metal would have retreated to $740/oz but then would recover to, once again, end the year higher than at the point which it had sat on January 1). But everyone who was losing faith in gold ignored factors which would sustain the yellow metal: global financial instability, rising costs in gold production along with insufficient (in number and size) new gold discoveries to replace that metal which was being pulled out of the ground.

'Gold has corrections and always will have. Get over it,' I wrote in an online commentary on April 3. 'As of this morning, the yellow metal was back at $900 an ounce. The only amazing aspect of all the commentary is that anyone was actually amazed at the correction.' But you would not be able to see that perspective if you had believed gold was a commodity. You wouldn't put pork bellies, zinc or live cattle in a safety deposit box. But people do put gold in the bank — that's why it is different.

Of course speculators were selling gold — it was one of the few things they could sell at a reasonable price. This coincided with news that hedge funds — one of the main sources of metal speculation at that time — were getting deeper and deeper into trouble. In *The Trillion Dollar Meltdown*, a book published around this time, author Charles R Morris had argued that finance sector write-downs that year would hit $1 trillion. Well, it did not happen quite like that. But even some true believers in the yellow metal were wavering. One of those was Marc Faber, whose title of 'Dr Doom' belies the fact that he often has something positive to say. This is the man who started buying gold in 2001, saying then the metal was going to rise. However, in early 2008 he wondered aloud whether gold could go as low as $750 in that present cycle. Then he went on to argue that the only way the U.S. could stave off a deep recession was just to keep printing money and eroding the value of the greenback still further. Gold must, in that eventuality, go higher, he argued. (By May 2015, as this was written, the Federal Reserve still did not have enough faith in the American economy's resilience to justify lifting interest rates off the floor.)

But, also that week, we heard from Evy Hambro, who ran the BlackRock mining fund out of London, and who pointed to gold shortages. On Bloomberg television he said this: 'Gold production peaked when gold was $250 an ounce back in 2001 and has been declining almost every year. Today's prices aren't high enough to encourage supply.' In the previous twenty years, there had been enormous technical advances in the gold sector — geochemistry, satellite imagery, larger ball mills — but gold production peaked in 2001 despite all this technology. (It increased in 2014, but not on a scale that makes all that much difference.) Gold producers were locked into high-energy consumption to make full use of these new mills, the huge new dump trucks and crushers. A high oil price in recent years caused immense pain to the gold industry, relieved only in 2015 when Saudi Arabia set out on its path to kneecap North American shale output by flooding the market and sending crude prices tumbling.

Following Hambro's comments out of Hong Kong came a speech delivered by Newmont Mining executive at a gold conference underway in Perth. Newmont's view was that the world was facing a diminishing level of major gold discoveries of a size greater than five million ounces; meanwhile, global output was running ahead of replacement by new reserves. Newmont's Tanami (Australia) operations manager, Adriaan van Kersen, told the conference there had been 'an alarming and decreasing trend in discoveries above one million ounces'. But, going back to Hambro's comment earlier, here's the thing: gold producers were able to lift production back when gold was worth $250/oz, but not when it was close to $1,000. That was a staggering situation. It was already getting hideously expensive just to find the stuff. (Again, in 2014, gold production was increasing but that was the delayed reaction to the big step-up in gold exploration that occurred once the industry realized price increases were there to stay and not, unlike the gold surge of 1980, a flash in the pan.)

2009: THEY'RE BUYING GOLD AGAIN

By early 2009 it was apparent that gold was being pulled two ways — in one way by physical demand, in the other by the derivatives market, the paper gold.

Any short selling even then belied what had been happening in the physical market. The Lipper Fund reported in 2009 that demand for physical gold rose by sixty-four per cent in 2008, with demand for coins and bars rising eighty-seven per cent. Yet, at the time, the gold price was falling: so a falling price was not necessarily a bad thing, and that is when canny investors moved in to acquire more metal. There is none of the classic deflationary response: that of waiting in the expectation the price will fall further. The strength of gold is that is not hard to get people to buy on the dips.

But it is true that each significant retreat in the gold price seems to throw up yet another question about the value of the 'safe haven' role of the yellow metal, and gives free rein to those who worry that maybe, perhaps, it is a just another commodity after all. Then, just in the nick of time, some new information comes to hand. In August 2009 it was the then latest Société Generale-GFMS report on official sector activity in gold. The headline message was that central bank sales were tailing off. Net official sector sales in the first six months of 2009 totalled thirty-nine tonnes, down seventy-three per cent on the same period in 2008. France, the biggest seller, was almost near the limit of what it could unload under the Central Bank Gold Agreement (CBGA); the next two biggest sellers were the European Central Bank and Sweden.

Then we had the news from China: it disclosed out of the blue that its central bank holdings had risen from the previously announced 600 tonnes to 1,054 tonnes. The report contained a revealing bar chart: it showed the holdings of gold as a percentage of total reserves. In the case of the U.S., gold accounted for about seventy-five per cent of official reserves. In the case of Europe, the average for members of the CBGA deal was just under sixty per cent. For the world as a whole, the average was around ten per cent. But China was a standout. Less than three per cent of Beijing's official reserves were in 2009 in the form of gold. True, this figure was so small simply because China's foreign exchange currency reserves were so huge — $2.09 trillion at that stage. (It was noted that, in early 2015, those official 1,054 tonnes at China's central bank by then represented just one per cent of the country's official reserves, another factor that made many believe that Beijing had obviously accumulated more gold since 2009.)

Even Société-Generale and GFMS, neither given to flights of imagination, in 2009 saw China buying more gold to insure itself against currency depreciation (highly sensible with the Federal Reserve's liquidity flood in the form of new U.S. dollars). But they doubted China would make any large purchase on the open market (such as bidding for gold then about to be sold off by the International Monetary Fund), expecting it to make discreet buys on its local gold market. Their view was that any large buys on the international market would scare the horses about the U.S. dollar, a matter of importance considering all those trillions of greenbacks in China's foreign reserves.

The other interesting development at that time was the decision by Venezuela on the amount of domestically produced gold that had to be delivered to the central bank in Caracas: this amount had just been increased from twenty per cent to *seventy* per cent of what the miners operating in Venezuela produced. Venezuela then stood at sixteenth place in the world in terms of its gold reserves. While the new rule was hardly likely to encourage gold mining there, it spoke volumes about that government's concern about relying on its U.S. dollar-denominated income from oil and gold.

By November 2010 — a month during which gold hit $1,420/oz — it was worth remarking that gold stocks were very much lagging the physical gold price. U.S. commentator Bill Fleckenstein put the situation thus: 'Gold stocks trade as though an attack of the swine flu or worse will infect anyone buying them.' Gold was looking great; the explorers not so much. They were struggling to raise enough money even with potentially world-class projects. As I remarked at the time in my column in *The Australian* newspaper, and paraphrasing Alan Greenspan, when it came to gold stocks, the market was exhibiting what might be called 'irrational equivocation'.

2010: GOLD BUBBLE?

It's December 2010, and The *Wall Street Journal* published an article warning investors not to be lured back into buying gold on the correction then under way. It's all over, was the message as the metal lost almost $80/oz in a few days (it would regain most of that by the time the month ended).

This followed a market summary from Ocean Equities in London showing that, over the previous ten years, gold's annual return had been 14.3 per cent (in Sterling terms) compared with 5.9 per cent a year from bonds and 1.6 per cent in cash terms. Here was the crusher: 'Equity returns were negative'. This did rather fly in the face of the gold-naysayers who were arguing gold was a passive investment. Well, maybe a gold bar just sits there but the gold price doesn't — or hasn't, or won't. The note continued: 'During periods of high inflation, gold returns are commensurately high'. This in a year after the base money supply in the United States rose by 100 per cent. As Nelson Bunker Hunt said: 'Almost anything is better than paper money … any fool can run a printing press'.

In 2010 George Soros stood up at the World Economic Forum's January 2010 meeting and called gold the 'ultimate asset bubble'.

2011: GOLD BEARS WAVER

As we went into 2011, though, the mood among many analysts and commentators seemed to change: they, too, seemingly became convinced that gold's rise was no flash-in-the-pan. But there was still a sizable body of them that still did not buy the gold story.

In January 2011, Pawel Rajszel, analyst at Toronto-based Veritas Investment Research, sent out a report arguing that gold shortages were over. As he noted, gold production had been dipping since 2001, but the 2009 performance by the global mining sector — its best year since 2003 — was showing a trend to rising output. Twenty of the world's top gold producers, which accounted for half the world's gold production, had aggressive growth plans, Rajszel said. They planned to increase production by twenty-five per cent through to 2013. In other words, he implied, there would be plenty to go around.

The other side of the coin came from the team at Standard Chartered in Hong Kong. And was a copper coin. A recent survey they had done showed that seventy-nine of eighty-one copper projects they had identified were running an average eighteen months late due to the global financial crisis. 'Why, you may ask, is that important for gold?' they continued. 'Simply because forty percent of the mined gold supply each year comes from copper mines as a by-product." Needless to say, the boys at Standard Chartered were now braced for another gold breakout. Also bullish were Swiss traders MKS Finance which was predicting 'another glorious year' for gold. It was calling an average $1,502/oz in 2011 for gold, $36.25/oz for silver. If that happened, I commented at the time, it would also represent a significant closing of the ratio between the two metals, a fascinating trend in itself.

Also in early 2011 — in April to be exact — several events were occurring in the United States that made some people think: the Chinese are consuming a huge proportion of the gold mined in the world. What if

Americans tried to do the same and suddenly began to hoard and relying on gold (and silver) as a store of wealth? There were signs by 2011 that this might have been ahead, and such a trend would have extraordinary ramifications for the gold price and must have a knock-on effect for gold producers.

By this stage of 2011, Utah's state legislature had passed a law that recognized federally issued gold and silver coins as legal tender (but not foreign minted coins). The legislation, incidentally, was called the Utah Sound Money Act, which revealed the mindset of its backer. Meanwhile, the lower house in Montana had then just rejected a bill that would allow people to pay state taxes in gold. The bill — which was a radical scheme based on the case that the states should lead the way in going back to the gold standard — was defeated by only four votes, fifty-two to forty-eight.

At then same time, then Texas congressman Ron Paul was campaigning in Washington to have gold and silver recognized as legal tender in America. All these developments signaled a growing uneasiness about the devaluation of the paper currency. Previously, all that talk of gold (and/or silver) as the only 'real' currency had long been confined to the precious metals enthusiasts and those convinced that you could not, when it came to the inflationary crunch, depend on paper money (a view underlined by memories of Weimar Germany).

Fast-forward to 2015. In Austin, Texas, Governor Greg Abbott signed into law a bill passed by the state legislature to build a state gold depository (by the House voting 140 to four, the Senate by twenty-five to four). The state wanted the gold it owns (5,600 bars worth $650 million) brought back from New York to somewhere it could get its hands on the bullion and make sure it was secure. The gold was not actually owned by the state, but by the University of Texas Investment Management Company, although you could see what they meant. Interestingly, it was reported that the endowment fund began buying gold in 2008 due to concern about what was described as 'excess monetization' (they meant money-printing) by central banks. However, Texan ambitions in 2015 went beyond those 5,600 bars: the depository would be available to anyone else wanting a safe place to store gold, putting Austin on the gold map.

2012: GOLD GAINS RESPECTABILITY

The gold standard has pretty well remained discredited since the 1930s. But, by 2012, discussion of some international financial yardstick was growing. The 2012 Republican Party convention authorized a committee being established to study the role of gold in the U.S. financial system. (At the 1896 convention, one of the issues which the eventual winner, William McKinley, had to face was the feeling among some delegates that he was not sufficiently committed to the gold standard.)

Then in 2012 the Basel Committee on Banking Supervision initiated a move to have gold changed from a Tier 3 banking asset — that is, banks being able to value their gold holdings at only fifty per cent of their worth — to a Tier 1 asset where the full value of the gold could be put on the bank's balance sheet. That did not eventuate but cannot be ruled out in the future.

Also in 2012 Savak Soharab Tarapore, who joined the Reserve Bank of India in 1961 as a research officer and retired in 1996 as deputy governor, and by now writing a regular column in that daily *The Hindu Business Line*, castigated what he called 'totally absurd policies' by so many governments in resorting to the printing presses to kick-start their economies. He said the U.S. dollar, the yen, the euro and the pound were all suspect currencies as a result of money creation. Tarapore urged the Reserve Bank of India to start buying gold as insurance. He pointed out that China intended to add 1,000 tonnes a year to its central bank's reserves. He did not say where he got this information. He then contrasted the holdings of developed countries with those of developing ones. At that time, the U.S. had seventy-seven per cent of its reserves in the form of gold, Germany seventy-four per cent, Italy seventy-three per cent. By contrast, Tarapore argued, the developing world held relatively little gold. Brazil had just one per cent of its reserves in gold, China and Malaysia two per cent, Taiwan six per cent, Russia and India nine per cent.

So what if these countries started buying more gold? What sort of further pressure was that going to put on availability of the physical metal? Tarapore continued: 'If all the major emerging economies were to raise, in unison, the proportion of gold in their reserves to say fifteen per cent, the demand for gold would be so high that gold prices would hit stratospheric levels of $3,000 a fine ounce or more. Apart from short-term fluctuations, there is absolutely no possibility of a retrenchment in the price of gold as central banks would step in and undertake purchases.'

Meanwhile, as Christmas 2012 was just a week or so away, the analysts were divided as ever about our yellow metal.

London-based Whitman Howard analyst Roger Bade had long been a gold bear, predicting the metal was doomed to fall back to around $1,000 an ounce. You could sense from his overnight note that he could barely contain his delight. 'Bang. Gold went straight through $1685/oz but found support just above $1660/oz and is now trying to recover around $1670/oz,' he wrote. 'It is becoming increasingly clear that gold might have been 2012's story; the recent rally in iron ore, Japanese hopes for uranium and rising polished diamond prices suggest new themes are developing for early 2013.' As mid-2015, the iron ore story was a busted flush, uranium and diamonds were still awaiting their days in the sun.

At the end of 2012 BlackRock — also based in the British capital — had a new argument against gold: shale (oil and gas). It took the view that America would see such resurgence from energy self-sufficiency that the U.S. dollar would once again become the envy of the world and we would forget all about that safe-haven, store-of-value thing.

By way of contrast, London's Capital Economics chief global economist Julian Jessop put out a note stating he was actually raising his gold forecast, from $2000/oz in late 2013 to $2200/oz. That did not happen either. 'Since gold is both expensive relative to its own history and provides no income, it is understandable that gold might now look less attractive to investors,' Jessop wrote. However, his short-term prognosis was correct: that interest rates would remain low, minimizing the opportunity cost of holding gold. Further large-scale asset purchases by central banks were foreseen — including by those of Japan, Britain and the U.S., which was a surprising forecast to this writer. As I commented at the time, surely the Bank of England would be a laughing stock, having sold all that metal at less than a quarter of the 2012 price.

Thailand, South Korea, Sri Lanka and Bangladesh had sent their central banks back buying into the gold market over the preceding twelve months, while Mexico's bought 100 tonnes in 2011.

In fact, that year saw world's central banks buy more bullion than at any time in almost fifty years — a net 536 tonnes. On top of that, there had been the much publicized move by the Bundesbank to bring home some of its gold stored abroad. The move to repatriate 300 tonnes from the Federal Reserve vaults in New York and all the 374 tonnes held at the Banque de France set off alarm bells among many gold observers that central banks no longer trusted each other — they might with with piles of dollars, euro or yen maybe but not with gold. The day after the Bundesbank announcement, Austria's central bank felt compelled to release a statement that it planned to hold onto all its 280 tonnes of gold (and in 2015 would decide to repatriate some of it back to Vienna).

It was at this time, too, that John Ing of Toronto-based Maison Placements Canada pointed out, gold was up 'only' 550 per cent from its lows of 2002 whereas from 1971 to 1980 it climbed by nearly 2,500 per cent. That, in 2012 terms, would have translated from around $300/oz in 2002 to a run up to $7,500/oz.

2013: THOUGHTS TURN TO GOLD MINERS

At the start of 2013, I posed the question in one of my regular columns as to how many directors of gold companies — explorers and miners — actually believed in the yellow metal. That is, did these directors like gold, did they really believe it was a form of money, probably the purest form of money? That was written before I came across an essay then having just been penned by Robert Cohen of the Toronto-based financial house GCIC. He took the issue of gold and mining companies into a new dimension.

What he was suggesting, in effect, was that gold mining companies retain some of their production and, in effect, become a quasi-exchange-traded fund. His essay was called 'Why miners should use gold as a functional currency'. Cohen was concerned that gold companies were selling their metal output for cash — the very opposite of what they should be doing, in his view. Over the previous decade printed money denominations had lost at least seventy per cent of their value. He cited the case of a Canadian house. In 1986, the selling price of that house was equivalent to 200 ounces of gold; in 2012, the selling price of that house was equivalent to 200 ounces of gold.

By mid-2013 gold was struggling. In June, the metal dropped from about $1,400/oz to just below $1,220/oz. It posed a very interesting conundrum regarding the future of gold supply with analysts worrying about further price falls leading to mine closures (a situation to which we returned in mid-2015).

At this stage we were (again) asking the vital question: the amount of gold in the world (above ground and refined) grows by something between one per cent and two per cent a year. What if it falls further as gold mines close? With a shortage of gold, what happens next? Will the price then have to rebound, and rebound substantially, just to encourage miners to go back into production? In 2013 this was a very real consideration. In June 2013, Marc Faber, the noted contrarian who edits the *Gloom, Boom and Doom Report*, made this point on a business television channel: 'Whereas gold is close to $1,300 compared to say $700 in 2008, conditions in the mining industry are horrible. The exploration companies are running out of money and industry conditions are worse than they were in 2008. So I think that a lot of supply that potentially comes to the market through new exploration will simply not be there. In emerging economies sovereign funds, central banks and individuals will continue to accumulate physical gold'.

Yet there were some unusual events occurring in gold trading at this time. When New York gold trading opened on 12 April 2013, 3.4 million ounces (or 110 tonnes) of June futures contracts were dumped on the market, sending the gold price plummeting. Two hours later, another ten million ounces (300 tonnes) hit the trading screens. One of Australia's most astute mining analysts, Warwick Grigor then of Canaccord Genuity (and now back running his own Far East Capital), commented at the time: 'This had all the hallmarks of a concerted short sale designed to break the back of the gold market. When a party dumps fifteen per cent of annual world mine supply it can only be for one purpose.' (Until then, Grigor had never espoused the manipulation theory, but he has been joined by other highly regarded gold analysts.)

Grigor's client note went on to make this point: the Fed's quantitative easing debased the value of the U.S. dollar. This made gold the stabilizing currency. But this was not what the Federal Reserve wanted. So bullion had been attacked with full force by U.S. monetary authorities working with the investment banks. And it had achieved its aim. 'The credibility of gold as a safe haven has been blown apart and it is now behaving like a commodity, open to manipulation in futures markets notwithstanding a strong physical market,' wrote Grigor. 'Confidence in the objectivity of markets has been a major casualty. Trust has been shattered.'

And the effects were soon being seen. London's *The Sunday Times* reported that 'global gold miners face a wave of big losses, mine closures and chief executive dismissals'. And *The Financial Times* noted that gold miners would be under pressure to write down assets once the then Federal Reserve chairman Ben Bernanke had flagged a tapering of quantitative easing. It was QE that supported global equity and with it the price of gold, the newspaper added.

(In July 2015 we had an eerily similar occurrence. At a time at which trading was normally quiet, someone dumped sell contracts totaling twenty-four tonnes on the Globex exchange in New York. At almost exactly the same time, another big quantity of gold contracts was dumped on the Shanghai Gold Exchange. It had the predictable consequence of sending the gold price plummeting to $1080/oz. Once again, I asked myself: if so many critics keep espousing the view that gold is a bad investment, surely this should be apparent to most investors; but it appears not to be, and so once again the big guns have to be brought to bear on the yellow metal — which rather suggests that gold is not quite the busted flush it is made out to be. These well-timed, and well-financed, attacks on gold suggest that someone out there fears it still.)

If all this disruption in 2013 was not bad enough, the World Gold Council was then about to release a new standard for reporting mining costs incurred producing the yellow metal. Until then, the industry had used the cash-cost method — which had not included capital spending, administrative costs, royalties, exploration costs and site rehabilitation costs (among others). The WGC's new all-in cost standard was to make it clear that many gold miners had in reality far higher costs per ounce that they had hitherto let on about. This was expected to make investment in gold stocks even less attractive. Yet, as one Australian commentator noted at the time, ten years earlier the industry was operating with prices at only about $400/oz and not too many gold miners went out of business then.

After all, did anyone think that a few government officials and investment bankers could just destroy a faith in gold that had lasted a long, long time? In fact, gold has been extracted from the ground for about 7,000 years and gold coinage became commonplace more than 3,500 years ago — and England's first gold sovereign was minted in 1489 AD.

But some perspective was needed. The declines in 2013 were by no means the most spectacular recorded. On 22 January 1980 gold crashed 17.6 per cent in one session. And at $763/oz on that day, the yellow one had a lot further to fall. By mid-1982 it was down about $300/oz. In June 2013, by contrast, it had taken the gold price two years to lose thirty per cent of its value. Part of the problem in 2013 was that the gold exchange-traded funds had unloaded more than 500 tonnes since the beginning of the year.

Within a few months, though, the gold story seemed to be back on the track. Japanese newspapers were reporting in September 2013 that the China renminbi (or yuan) was increasingly being used for trade settlements — in the first half of the year, China settled 2.05 trillion yuan ($334.8 billion) of its trade transactions in its own currency. That was a 16.1% slice of all trade by China.

To by-pass the U.S. dollar, China had by this time concluded currency swap contracts with other countries, including Australia, Brazil, Russia, Iran and Britain (the Bank of England being the first top central bank to allow currency swaps with the yuan). Beijing had also created a new oil wholesale structure that would bypass the petrodollar. As one commentator remarked, this was the first time in forty years that there had been a challenge to the dollar's hegemony.

Reports at about the same time included an item in a South African business newspaper (reputed for its coverage of the mining industry) saying Chinese companies were on a buying spree for gold projects — a trend that was soon to become very much more apparent. In June that year, 106.4 tonnes of gold was imported by China through Hong Kong. So, in month, China imported more gold than Canadian mines produced in a year. In the first six months, Chinese imports totalled 706 tonnes: that was the annual combined production from the No. 2 through No. 4 gold producing countries in the world — that was equivalent to a whole year's mining in Australia, the United States and Russia; and these imports were on top of China's own production, the largest in the world. The Bangkok daily *The Nation* concluded: 'China is apparently preparing to adopt a gold standard'. It also reported that 'speculation is widespread that (China) could be holding between 7,000 and 10,000 tonnes, surpassing the U.S. (official reserves of) 8,113 tonnes'.

On August 5, 2013, an official from the People's Bank of China, Yao Yudong, wrote an article in the *China Securities Journal* arguing a new 'Bretton Woods' agreement was needed — and one that created a new gold-backed reserve currency to replace what he termed as the dying dollar. In late 2013 *China Daily* reported that countries in Central Asia along with Pakistan were in discussions with Beijing to have currency swap arrangements. Trade between the Central Asian republics and China hit $40 billion the previous year.

Malaysia was not buying the 'gold is dead' story, either. In October 2013 the country's stock exchange, the Bursa Malaysia, began trading gold futures. The 100-gram, ringgit-denominated contract was to allow investors to trade without worrying about currency fluctuations, said Chong Kim Seng, chief executive officer of Bursa Malaysia Derivatives. (The ringgit is the Malaysian currency.) So Kuala Lumpur joined Singapore, Taipei,

Shanghai and Hong Kong as Asia gold futures trading centres. With the Malaysian contract, the investor needed only RM1,000 ($255 at mid-2015 exchange rates) to start trading. All contracts were to be cash-settled; there was no delivery of physical gold. (Which reminds us that $250 billion gold derivatives are traded globally every day, greater that the volume of Sterling Gilts or German Bunds. Another part of the derivatives time-bomb is therefore ticking away; just hope not everyone wants to trade their paper for physical gold all the same time.)

Also at that time Bangkok's *The Nation* reported that Singapore had been trying to persuade Thailand's top five gold traders to establish footholds in the city-state as it aimed to become a centre for gold-price referencing in Southeast Asia. The newspaper reported Nuttapong Hirunyasiri, managing director of MTS Gold Futures, saying the Singapore government had dispatched a team to Thailand to offer relaxed regulations and tax incentives to traders who open offices in that country.

Consumer gold demand in Thailand had risen fifty-eight per cent in the June 2013 quarter (compared to the three months to June 30, 2012). While India and China imported the largest tonnages, Thailand — while number three in absolute tonnages — actually at that time came in at number one in Asia on imports of gold per capita.

According to *The Financial Times*, Singapore — not content with being a regional hub for trading coal, iron ore and crude oil — was aiming to do the same with gold. During 2012, in what was clearly in preparation for this move, Singapore abolished sales taxes on imports of investment-grade gold and other precious metals. Then, in 2013, Switzerland's Metalor Technologies opened a refinery in Singapore with the aim of producing 360 tonnes of gold bars a year. Trade Minister Lim Hng Kiang said Singapore wanted to capture between ten and fifteen per cent of the world's bullion trade. And there was an interesting point in *The Financial Times* report: while the world had been watching Chinese gold imports through Hong Kong, about a fifth of Beijing's gold purchases were by 2013 being routed through Singapore, which indicated China was importing even more gold than we had thought.

2.
WHAT HISTORY TEACHES
US ABOUT GOLD

FOR ONE THING, DEFLATION as well as inflation can cause conditions in which gold is an attractive acquisition. The inflation case is clear: gold, rather than paper money, maintains its value. But, anyway, let's daydream for just a few moments about a world where gold is the one trusted store of wealth (as it was during the Great Depression). Gold's role in deflation was amply demonstrated by Homestake Mining which saw its shares rise each year between 1929 and 1935 and so, too, its dividends to shareholders. During the six years of the Great Depression, Homestake Mining paid out $128 per share in dividends. If you bought Homestake Mining shares from your Wall Street broker in October 1929 they cost $80, but by 1935 Homestake stock was worth $495 per share.

But there was also another big story of the time that should resonate and bring comfort to the gold sector — the formation in March 1933 of what would become one of the giants of Australian mining, Western Mining Corporation. Remember: this was possibly the worst year of the slump, the Dow Jones by the end of 1932 having lost eighty-two per cent of its worth since the 1929 crash.

The month before Western Mining was formed, newspapers were reporting frenzied excitement on the London Stock Exchange focused on buying shares in South African gold miners. By 1934, when Homestake stockholders were raking in the dividends, Western Mining had established its Gold Mines of Kalgoorlie operation, based in the Western Australian gold mining centre. A year later, there would be its Central Norseman Gold.

The depression, and the increased value of gold, had an extraordinary effect on the industry in Australia. According to the 1935 Australian Year Book, the value of the gold yield in the country in 1929 was the lowest recorded since the discovery of the metal in 1851. There was a slight increase in production in 1930 as gold prospecting started to pick up and operators looked to start working over old mining areas.

But then the price of gold paid to miners started to get a move on.

Anyone born before 1960 will be able to follow the pounds/shillings/pence amounts (the quarter fractions refer to farthings) and, of course, know that a pound then was real money; you didn't break a pound note lightly.

For those born later, there are conversions in parentheses — the amounts bear no relation to today's values, but you'll get the picture.

* Australian miners earned £5/19/9d ($11.98) an ounce in 1931.
* In 1932 the gold was worth £7/5/11¾ an ounce (around $15.60).
* In 1933 it rose slightly to £7/14/3¾.
* Then in 1934, the price was £8/10./0¼ (around $17).

London-based Wiluna Gold Corp (mining in Australia) in 1934 paid a dividend equivalent to 22.5 per cent of the face value of its £1 shares.

What you have to remember is that, in parallel with this substantial increase in the gold price, prices of almost everything else – labour, fuel, food, etc. – were actually falling (that is, deflation), which must have significantly improved the margins for the mining companies (as has the falling oil price now). In 1933 the American Bureau of Metal Statistics estimated that 1932 worldwide production of gold totalled at least 23.5 million ounces worth $485.7 million, compared with 21.33 million ounces in 1931, 20.3 million ounces in 1930 and 19.86 million ounces in 1929. (The 1932 figure was probably higher as the Americans were working with old figures on Russian output but anecdotal evidence suggested those figures had been surpassed.) But what is significant is that the price kept rising during the slump in the face of not only increasing mine production but the sudden surge in scrap supplies.

Gold recycled from jewellery and other items soared as owners needed money. In the year to September 1932, British India exported the equivalent of 11.5 million ounces salvaged from fabricated items. Germany was another big source of gold from scrap.

In other words, the world in the 1930s just could not get enough gold.

Long before people began to think about, and worry about, deflation as the 2008 global financial crisis hit, a hedge fund consultant named Sam

in 1996 had written a paper (*The Behaviour of Gold Under Inflation*) showing that, in every instance of deflation since President Andrew Jackson, Americans had preferred gold to paper money.

He studied the deflationary periods following the panics of 1837 (after land speculation), 1857 (post-railway construction), 1869 (Civil War finance), 1873 (railway construction), 1893 (Free Silver Movement), 1920 (post-Great War commodity boom), 1929 (the stock market collapse) and 1931 (the panic as the Great War debt imploded due to the worldwide depression). In all those, as Hewitt explained, gold was linked the U.S. dollar, the fixed-rate exchange mechanism. As he pointed out, since the United States had not experienced deflation since the operation of floating exchange rates, he had to dig deeper to find any potential parallels.

Of the historic deflationary episodes he reviewed, currency hoarding was a common feature as individuals focused on capital preservation. But they always preferred gold to paper money because gold did not represent the liability of any institution, and therefore was (is) unique among currency alternatives.

But most turned to gold only after the various bubbles had burst.

In 1932, when severe deflation was kicking in, people not only hoarded gold – they wanted to dig more out of the ground. 'Never before has the world been so thoroughly grubbed for gold,' reported *Time* magazine on 12 December 1932. Old time prospectors swarmed to abandoned goldfields and minor gold rushes were reported to be happening in Australia, South Africa, Chile, the Philippines and Venezuela.

In February 1933, *The Wall Street Journal* reported the world mine production in 1932 had reached a new record of 23.9 million ounces – up 7.8 per cent on 1931 output, and valued at $494.2 millions. Not only that, India had unlocked much of its gold reserves to meet global demand for the metal; it was estimated that British India between 1873 and 1931 had accumulated gold worth as much as £600 million (which is about £32.5 billion in 2015 pounds). South Africa dominated production with its mines turning out 11.56 million ounces in 1932. Next came Canada with just over three million ounces. The United States and the Soviet Union were third and fourth. (Russian output was growing apace under Stalin's urging: upwards of twenty dredges had been installed at alluvial deposits over the previous five years.

By the end of 1933, the *Los Angeles Times* was reporting that California had embarked upon a new era of gold mining, and there were more than 800 mines operating in the state with around 12,000 men prospecting in the mountainous areas. This was in spite of the federal government banning private ownership of the metal. (President Roosevelt's Executive Order 6102 forced Americans to hand over their gold to the government and made the possession of monetary gold by any individual, partnership, association or corporation a criminal offence.)

At the start of 1933, *Barron's* noted that, in 1932, not only had the world produced more gold than ever before, the central bank holdings rose to their highest level ever. As of January 1, 1933, the US and France between them held 61.5% of the world's gold stocks and European central banks were keen to retrieve their bullion stored with those two countries. In the first quarter of 1932, Washington repatriated 23.3 per cent of gold under its care.

Austria passed an emergency law forbidding gold being taken out of the country. The government even banned dental supply houses buying the metal (dentists were being used by investors and speculators as a front to buy the metal legally). Italy launched a 'battle of gold' to encourage people to turn over their metal in return for paper money.

The surge in gold demand also led to increasing speculation in gold shares. In New York, Alaska Juneau shares went from $11 to $15 in late 1932 — not as spectacular a gain as that of Homestake Mining shares but not bad considering the state of the U.S. stock market.

In May 1932 *The Mail* (then an Adelaide newspaper) reported that 'in times of trade depression, increased attention was being paid to gold mining in Australia' and shares in those miners had been doing well, too.

Gold production was also helped by improved ore treatment, the reduction in costs of machinery and labour due to the depression, as well as by the League of Nations predicting that by 1940 the world's gold production would be in serious decline.

True, none of this is going to happen again. But what 1932 did show was that gold marches to its own drumbeat and that it can always do something quite different from what you might expect.

But there is a qualification to this discussion about production of gold. In 2012 Austria's Erste Bank issued a report on the metal that made this statement: 'Annual production is of relatively little significance to the pricing of gold'. As in most things economic, one bows to the Austrians. The team of analysts in Vienna argued that there had been an elementary misunderstanding about gold. Too many investors and analysts (and journalists, presumably) attached too much importance to annual production and annual demand. Gold is all alone in one respect: 'To the buyer, it makes no difference whether the gold was produced three weeks or three millennia ago.' Every gram of gold held anywhere in the world was for sale — at a price. And the supply side? Gold lasts, it endures down the ages, and most of the gold that has been mined since before records existed is still around. The recycling of existing gold accounts for a much larger share of supply than is the case for other commodities, said the bank. With only a small amount consumed for industrial use, most of the gold ever produced was still available. With (an estimated) 170,000 tonnes available, what difference does a few hundred tonnes make, the analysts asked.

Here is another argument out of Austria. Gold is not precious because there is too little of it. The reason is more subtle: gold is precious because annual production is so low relative to the stock still in existence. Gold has acquired this feature over many centuries and cannot lose it. Commodities are consumed. Gold is hoarded.

But the Erste report also contained some disquieting news for gold miners. There was a widely held view that gold could not drop below a certain level – say, $1000/oz – because that level of pricing would force so many mines to close, which would mean an even greater shortage of gold, which would send the price back up. Not so fast, said our Austrian friends. The trade of existing gold — far and away much greater in tonnages than what comes out of the ground each year — would not be affected by a number of mines closing. The mining sector therefore had little influence on the gold price.

The demand side is made up of investors, the jewellery industry, central banks and the industrial sector. But this is just a fraction of total demand. No, the largest part of demand is accounted for by reservation — in other words, gold owners who do not want to sell gold at whatever is the price of the gold. 'This means the decision not to sell at current prices is as important as the decision to buy gold,' Erste analysts argued. In fact, the supply of recycled gold had increased only marginally since 2009 in spite of a drastic increase in the gold price. 'This distribution indicates that gold holdings are gradually moving from weak to strong hands,' the bank said.

And that is why gold is going from the weak hands of the West to the strong hands of China. Western companies mine it and sell it, China buys it and hoards it.

But the present developments are just one more example of how, in relatively short periods of time, the gold industry undergoes significant changes. And that holds just as true over longer periods, too. During the Middle Ages, the main suppliers of gold were Saxony, Austria and Spain. Then the Spaniards and Portuguese colonized Central and South America, leading those territories to become important mining locations.

Between 1761 and 1840 Russia began to overtake Mexico and Brazil. After 1841, California and Australian gold finds changed the balance yet again and, with Russia still powering along, the world's gold production leapt to the equivalent of 140 tonnes a year. Then Africa took over the lead. By the 1930s the Rand goldfields had been providing half the world's gold for a decade. Australia was No. 6 on the list in 1934 — behind Africa, Canada, the United States, the Union of Soviet Socialist Republics, and the Japanese Empire. These were the geographical terms used by the American Council's Institute of Pacific Relations.

In 1934 the institute prepared a report on gold production, the study provoked by the fact that the Great Depression had spurred many unemployed men to start searching for gold, with prospecting 'pushed energetically in Siberia, Australia, New Zealand, Japan, Canada and Kenya'.

By this time, Californian output was falling off (U.S. peak gold output had been reached in 1915) but Alaska was the second largest American area of production. But the report noted that 'there has been no single major discovery of gold in the United States for twenty-five years', and the authors expected the country's gold supply to depend heavily on extracting it as a by-product of other metals.

By this time, too, deposits in Japan (which had seen gold mining from ancient times) were close to exhaustion but production was increasing in Taiwan (which had been ruled from Tokyo since the 1894 Sino-Japanese War).

The report noted that Australia, in terms of its share of world production, was in decline with the emergence of Canada, Russia and Africa. Australia in 1870 had produced 35.5 per cent of global gold. But the authors noted recent discoveries in Western Australia and concluded: 'It is believed that the country will continue to rank among the leaders in gold production'. As indeed it has.

The institute saw what was then New Guinea (being a former German territory, it was a League of Nations mandate and still separated administratively from Papua) as a coming star what with the opening up of the country by air services. Then there was the Philippines: early Chinese called the Philippines 'Land of Gold' and by the 1930s there was a strong belief that mining might help the economic development of the islands. And they believed that the Netherlands Indies (now Indonesia) 'may play an important part supplying world needs'.

And now, in 2015, we have a new player, albeit a small one.

Irish newspapers were excited about a gold find near the border between Northern Ireland and the republic. Three feet from surface in County Monaghan, Dublin-based Conroy Gold & Natural Resources reported a gold-bearing area 700m by 300m. The discovery was within a fifty kilometer-long area stretching over three countries which the company believed was a new gold province and Conroy has set itself a target of finding possibly as much as twenty million ounces. At the time, Conroy was one of three Toronto-listed companies with high hopes of Irish gold.

Actually, Ireland has quite a history with gold. Artifacts testify to the mining and fabricating of gold in prehistoric times on the island. Ireland had its own Bronze Age (2500BC until 700BC) and gold nuggets were found in the Moyola River in 1657. But in the past hundred years or more, very little was done to revive gold mining.

⁂

By 1942 gold was being mined at peak rates and taking labour, equipment and shipping space needed elsewhere. *Time* magazine harrumphed that the British Empire had 500,000 workers employed producing gold, while the United States had 55,000. As to the latter, President Roosevelt would soon see to that: in 1942 he ordered closed all gold mines in the country on the grounds that mining gold was not a war priority.

For Britain, though, gold was very much a priority. Britain needed gold with which to buy U.S. dollars; the Americans, on the other hand, needed copper, zinc and lead — but not gold. After all, Britain was paying its bills to Washington partly in the yellow metal so Roosevelt could afford the luxury of closing domestic mines (and also ban export of mining equipment to foreign gold companies). Of the half million subjects of the empire engaged in gold mining, four-fifths of that number were in South Africa (and other thirty-eight thousand in Canada — something else that rankled with *Time*).

When war broke out in 1939, South Africa was the premier gold producer of Africa with output reaching its peak in 1941 at 408 tonnes. Other important gold producers were Southern Rhodesia (now Zimbabwe), Gold Coast (Ghana), Belgian Congo (Democratic Republic of Congo), and Tanganyika (Tanzania). Almost all of South Africa's wartime production of gold was shipped to Britain. It was needed to bolster reserves and offset trade deficits.

But, as with so many other aspects of the war effort (military, political and economic), there was friction between Great Britain and the United States. The former placed great emphasis on keeping the South African gold mines going to help pay London's bills; the latter tried to apply pressure on Johannesburg to divert manpower and spending to the production of strategic metals.

As was the case with many commodities where the Imperial government dominated output, the price of gold was fixed from 1940 until 1945; at the same time, the miners were suffering from the rising costs of all their imported inputs. Once Britain was no longer desperate for gold with which to pay its bills (when Lend-Lease was extended), gold prospecting was banned in the East African colonies, and the mining companies were denied priority for machinery. Moreover, labour was scarce. The impact of Lend-Lease hit the gold industries in both Kenya and Tanganyika; only since the 1990s have they begun once again to grow significantly.

But, of course, the South African gold industry had its own problems. White skilled workers and supervisors were going off to war, many of the machinery works that serviced the gold miners' equipment were turned over to make munitions or other war materiel and — a problem that would get worse as the decades wore on — mining operations had to go ever deeper (and more expensively) as the more easily won, shallow gold was worked out.

Overall, though, gold production fell as the war progressed; in 1944, only about two-thirds of the amount of gold was being produced as in 1940. However, the American pressure for more strategic metals did have some effect: South Africa lifted output of not only platinum (needed in such things as spark plugs) but also of chrome, manganese, vanadium and copper.

HEDGING

Gold experienced short-term volatility back in the 1980s that sent the metal to its then all-time high (and in real terms, still its highest point) and then right back down again. Then along came hedging, which grew apace in the 1990s as the gold price sank and explorers and producers desperately locked in forward sales at the best prices they could get.

'Hedging was like pouring oil on troubled waters,' said veteran Sydney-based gold analyst, Keith Goode in a paper he wrote on the subject. So much gold was covered by these forward contracts that it took much of the skittishness out of the market. In 2001, when gold finished the year at $278.10/oz, companies had more than 100 million ounces of metal hedged. As 2006 opened with the gold price on 2 January at $519/oz, the hedge book total was down to about 50 million ounces. And they kept on de-hedging; surprisingly, even with the (relative) gold weakness since 2013, hedging has never staged a significant comeback. So we are back to business as usual in terms of volatility.

But here's another nuance: the volatility that returned as hedging declined did mean we saw some dramatic movements during the recent gold price boom. In 2009 there was a one-day fall of 4.01 per cent; on 13 June 2006, there was a plunge of 7.3 per cent in one trading session. But 2008 was the whopper: if you take gold's ten biggest one-day falls, six of those happened in 2008, the year the metal retraced to nearly $700/oz. But the yellow metal finished 2008 at $881, and the next year the metal broke through $1,200/oz. Here is the bottom line: however violent those down movements, they did not interrupt the overall price growth over the ten year period.

But look at the (really) long-term picture. Since December 31, 1799, only three decades have witnessed any significant declines in the gold price. Two of those lasted from 1980 after the price dropped from that year's record of $850/oz, through all the 1980s and 1990s, until the metal began easing upwards again in 2001.

The previous period was from 1864 until 1879, and that gold bust was due to a restoration of fiscal probity after the money printing during the U.S. Civil War. Before that war, the U.S. government issued no paper money: all its issuances were in gold, silver and copper coins. But to finance the war, the Lincoln administration introduced the greenback and printed $450 million worth of them. The Confederate states increased their money in circulation more than eleven-fold.

It was a pale harbinger of where we are now, but back then no wonder gold went from $20.67/oz in 1861 to $53.35/oz in 1864. Once the war — and the money printing — was over, gold fell again because the gold backing allowed trust to return to money.

⸎⸎⸎⸎⸎

One final point about inflation: the Weimar Germany experience (stories such as needing a wheelbarrow to transport the quantity of notes needed to buy a few items of food, for example) has been well documented and is well known (especially by gold followers) but there have been more recent and dramatic examples of how paper money can lose its attraction.

Inflation stalked parts of Europe as the Second World War ended. At the 1945 annual meeting in London of the Ottoman Bank, Colonel E.

Gore Browne described to shareholders how the Germans had systematically encouraged inflation in Greece. After the liberation, new drachma were issued at the equivalent of one to 50 billion of the old. At first, the new currency was fixed at 600 to the pound sterling, but by 1945 this had been adjusted to 2,000 to the pound.

In the week after the liberation, *Time* magazine on 13 November 1944 described the Greek financial system as lying prostrate. Finance minister Alexander Svolos tried to instil confidence in his country, citing the $175 million in gold reserves although the government could not get its hands on the yellow metal. No one was listening, apparently; *Time* reported that the value of a British gold sovereign rose from ten trillion drachmas to twenty-two trillion. Shopkeepers closed up, unwilling to sell for drachmas in return. Bartering was back. Bread sold for eleven billion drachmas a loaf.

Inflation was a fact of life as the war came to an end, and the money printing had been prodigious. Notes in circulation over the span of the war rose sharply: according to the League of Nations in 1945, note circulation in Greece was up more 312,422,000 per cent; even in non-belligerent Uruguay, money in circulation rose by twenty-five per cent. In Italy, Finland, Iceland, the Middle East, India and Japan the range was between 500 and 1,000 per cent. In the Baltics and Greece, paper money was losing its role as a means of payment. Croatia resorted to a barter system with farmers being paid for their produce in salt, cigarettes, tobacco and matches. In Syria, wholesale prices between July 1939 and December 1943 were up 800 per cent; in Turkey, a non-belligerent, prices rose close to 600 per cent by the end of 1943, although they started declining as 1944 wore on. Indian prices were up, in 1943, by 253 per cent on what they had been in 1939.

Greece's hyperinflation was but a curtain-raiser for what was to come in Hungary. When Weimer Germany finally took action against its now infamous period of hyperinflation, the rate of conversion from old to new currency was at the rate of one trillion to one. In Hungary's case, in August 1946, the new notes were issued at the exchange rate of four hundred octillion to one. Whereas inflation had been a widespread problem after the 1914-18 war, only Hungary had a repeat episode after the Second World War.

As with its Weimar precursor, the hyperinflation in Hungary began at what would later seem a modest pace. By June 1946, that pace became more frenetic. The *Manchester Guardian* in June 1946 described inflation as having reached 'fantastic heights'. In 1939 a loaf of bread had cost one-tenth of a pengo, the currency which had been introduced in 1927 to replace the then highly inflated korona; by June 1945, bread was costing one pengo. In April 1946, the equivalent amount of bread would have set you back ninety-six million pengo.

On the third day of January 1946, a correspondent of the *Christian Science Monitor* told his American readers that, because Hungarian notes were basically worthless, the only means by which to buy food was through barter. Parents in the city were sending their children to villages where food was available, the youngsters being provided with salt or boxes of matches to exchange for meals. By this time most city dwellers were existing on bread. Reporter R. H. Markham met a friend who he described as one of the most highly paid officials in Hungary. This fellow's family breakfasted on sugarless artificial tea, bread or potatoes, a tiny pat of butter and unsweetened jam. Lunch and supper consisted of soup and vegetables. The problem for government employees was that prices had increased roughly one hundred times faster than their salaries. The previous October, the Hungarian Prime Minister Bela Miklos received by way of monthly salary the amount of sixty-three thousands pengos; by January, that sum was insufficient to pay for a kilogram of apples.

Hungary, having joined the Axis powers, was forced in January 1945 to agree to pay reparations to the Soviet Union, Yugoslavia and Czechoslovakia to the tune of $300 million. But a more serious problem was that the taxation system broke down, and in the immediate post-war period only about ten per cent of government spending was covered by revenue collections. Borrowing had begun as soon as the pro-Nazi government fled Hungary taking the note printing plates and paper with them.

The stabilisation program ushered in the florint — the Hungarian rendering of the florin, which had been the currency of the Austro-Hungarian empire. You could collect a new florint at the bank by turning up with four hundred octillion pengos. Hungary was also able to recover twenty-two tonnes of gold that had been stolen by the Nazis; it was delivered to Buda-pest in Adolf Hilter's former private train. Tax rates were hiked — and made punitive to investors, with an eighty per cent rate on property income while companies were made to pay tax on revenues rather than profitability. By the end of 1946, ninety-six per cent of government spending was covered by government revenues.

In tandem with putting the brakes in inflation, the government went to great efforts to get goods into shops. William A. Bomberger and Gail E. Makinen in a 1980 article for an academic journal recount one transaction trail:

> Large quantities of Hungarian tobacco products, e.g., were sold in Vienna, where their price was high in dollars. The dollars were used to purchase cheap Polish sugar. The sugar was sold in Bucharest where its price was high in broken gold. The gold was taken to Budapest where it was struck by the Hungarian mint into gold Napoleons. These gold coins were then used to buy imported goods from Switzerland.

Another lesson about gold.

3.

GOLD IS MONEY

IF GOLD IS A commodity, and as such judged solely by its practical uses, it should be worth very little — less than silver, possibly, which has many industrial uses. If gold is just another commodity, then why is it worth more than $1,000 an ounce? Because there are still enough people in the world who believe that, when times get bad, gold will retain its value while economies deflate or inflate, bottoms fall out of the housing market and global instability surges. I am sorry that this all sounds very basic, very 'Investing 101'. But — it seems to me — that a basic point has been overlooked in all the arguing and handwringing about gold. There is nothing, repeat nothing, to justify gold being $1,000 (or $400 or even $200) other than a belief that, in the end, it is the ultimate store of value.

The gold enthusiasts live in hope that we are turning the full circle back to 550 BC when King Croesus of Lydia, located in what now is Turkey, struck the world's first gold coin, which circulated through many countries and was accepted as value.

Even when paper money came into being many centuries later, you could present those pieces of paper and ask for the equivalent in gold. When the Bank of England introduced bank notes in 1694 they came with a promise that the paper could be presented at the bank and the bearer could be handed gold to the equivalent value. (Try doing that with a pile of your local banknotes these days.)

In 50 BC Roman citizens began using a gold coin called the aureus, but it took the Norman invasion of 1066 for metallic currency to be used in what is today Britain. In 1284 England issued its own gold coin, the florin. Jump forward to 1792 when the Coinage Act established gold and silver as the basis for the U.S. currency system. The U.S. dollar was defined as being worth 24.75 grains of gold or 371.25 grains of silver.

In the modern era, there was the gold standard where paper money was convertible into gold. A country could print only as much money as could be backed by its gold. It was a dreadful straitjacket (much like the euro is today with countries like Spain, Latvia and Italy all having to use the same valued currency as the Germans and Dutch.)

The end of the gold standard tarnished the reputation of using the metal as a means of regulating money supply. But there are those who argue it needed changing, not abolishing. In 2010 World Bank boss Robert Zoellick wrote an article in *The Financial Times* of London suggesting a return of the gold standard, albeit as a hybrid including major currencies and commodities, to provide a stable measure of worth of paper money. The World Bank president was talking about a new-style Bretton Woods system, using gold as a reference point of market expectations as to inflation, deflation and currency values. Zoellick was careful how he phrased it, and he was certainly not calling for a return to the gold standard as it had been applied until the 1930s. This article released the genie: what had thus far been a subject only on those way-out gold websites was suddenly something you could discuss in polite company.

Winston Churchill's return to the gold standard in 1925 had been doomed to fail because it set the value of the pound at its pre-war gold price but inflation in the 1914-18 period had not been factored in. Similarly with the cost of the Vietnam war (and the consequent need to print money) that forced Richard Nixon to cut the last link, the commitment by the United States Treasury to pay other central banks $35 for each ounce of gold.

By 2010, few were suggesting a return to the Churchillian-style rigour of the gold standard; what many were suggesting, however, was some form of standard that would constrain governments and central banks inflating their way out of trouble and causing immense damage to personal savings.

But many saw the ending of the gold link to the U.S. dollar as a terrible financial decision. As Charles Kadlec commented in *Forbes* magazine: Today, August 15, 2011, is the fortieth anniversary of President Richard Nixon's colossal error: severing the final link between the dollar and gold. No other single action by Nixon has had a more profound and deleterious effect on the American people. In the end, breaking the solemn promise that a dollar was worth 1/35th of an ounce of gold doomed his Presidency, and marked the beginning of the worst forty years in American economic history.

Kadlec argued that unemployment thereafter averaged six per cent, whereas between 1945 and 1971 the average was five per cent. In 1975, the jobless numbers hit 8.5 per cent, far higher than for even the worst of the post-war years leading up to 1971. He calculated that economic growth had lost one per cent over the forty years since 1971, denying Americans $8 trillion in total and the chance to lift median family income to $70,000 a year.

To the *Kansas City Star*, the appropriate headline for the fortieth anniversary of the Nixon move was 'Disaster followed leaving the gold standard' over an article pointing to the legacy of forty years of inflation. That legacy included gold having gone from $35/oz to over $1,700/oz at the time of that being written (what better example of inflation than that?) but that we now tolerate inflation rather than having (as would have happened in the old days) our financial authorities beat it back with a fiscal stick. A writer in *The Wall Street Journal* took the contrary view. 'Gold standard: forty years gone – and good riddance'. (On 25 July 2015, just before gold bounced, the *Washington Post* headlined 'Gold is Doomed".)

In that same week in 2011 as the media remembered the events of forty years earlier, there were signs that perhaps the world was getting back some sort of gold standard by stealth. *The Financial Times* pointed out that gold was reclaiming its place at the heart of the global financial system, the most striking evidence (apart from its price) being that central banks had by then turned on a dime and were buying up gold rather than dumping it. In the first six months of 2011, net central bank buying reached 208 tonnes of gold, the highest since 1981. Ambrose Evans-Pritchard, the highly regarded commentator at London's *The Daily Telegraph*, had weeks before begun the ball rolling with a piece titled 'Return of the gold standard as world order unravels'. He suggested a new gold standard would probably be based on a variant of the Bancor idea proposed by Keynes in the 1940s, who suggested a supranational currency — the bancor — which was backed by gold to be used in trade between countries (although Keynes proposed you would still use your drachma, lire or peso at the corner store). Operated by what he called an International Clearing Union, countries with trade deficits would be forced to reduce the value of their currencies while those with large trade surpluses would be obliged to revalue upwards.

Back in 2009, the head man at the Bank of China, Zhou Xiaochuan, gave a speech in which he talked about the bancor idea, calling it 'far-sighted', and suggesting the International Monetary Fund be equipped to operate a similar scheme. If there was a bancor-style system, the Americans could not have had the succession of quantitative easings (money printing) and the European Central Bank could not have broken its own rules and bought Italian bonds to prop up that member country.

But such a system might not necessarily be good for gold. The new system would ensure that panic subsided, prudence reigned and suddenly there would no urgency to own gold. There would be an obvious strong demand for gold — the central banks would buy more, obviously. But, without the panic factor, they might expect to be able to do so at, say, $950/oz (pluck a figure out of the air). That's not a prospect our gold miners would cherish.

But, as we are not likely to see such a system, gold retains its store of value appeal.

In modern times, the greatest blows delivered against gold came from the White House. In 1933, Franklin D. Roosevelt banned all private holdings of gold; then in 1942 he ordered closed all U.S. gold mines, as he considered the production of gold non-essential to the war effort.

On 9 March 1933, the United States Congress — at the behest of Roosevelt, who had been sworn in just five days earlier — passed the Emergency Banking Act. It authorized the government to confiscate all privately held gold, some $1.4 billion of it. If you did not turn in your bullion to the Feds you laid yourself open to ten years in prison and a $10,000 fine. Department of Justice agents banged on the doors of those they suspected of holding gold. Frederick Barber Campbell, a New York lawyer, was the first American to be indicted for failure to report his holdings of gold to the U.S. Treasury. He had twenty-seven gold bars deposited at the Chase National Bank, then worth $200,500, according to newspaper reports. The bank was refusing to return his gold on Campbell's demand due to the new law. Campbell had brought the prosecution upon himself to test the act of Congress, and he had sought a restraining order on Chase National to prevent it handing the gold over to the Federal Reserve. Campbell's case was that there had not been due process of law. He lost his case.

(It was estimated at this time that some $11.2 billion worth of gold was being hoarded around the world. The greatest hoarders were the French, said to be holding gold worth $4.1 billion.)

There is disagreement about why Roosevelt did it. Some argue he wanted the gold to back the U.S. dollar, others say it was so he could have no limit on credit creation once gold was out of private hands and fiat paper currency was the only means of payment and representative of money.

There were historical precedents. Lenin confiscated privately held gold in 1921, but that was simply to be able to have enough to pay the bills. In Weimar Germany, hit in 1923 by hyperinflation, gold was also taken out of private hands. As recounted by Adam Fergusson, in his 1975 title, *When Money Dies* (reissued in 2010), on 8 September 1923 the Berlin government appointed a Commissioner for the Control of Foreign Exchange. He was give power to seize not only foreign currency to help meet the country's foreign exchange needs but gold securities. The commissioner also seized physical gold, silver, platinum and alloys, whether in coin or raw material. As Fergusson noted, 'Germany's gold reserves were effectively down to the equivalent of £14 million, too little now with which to establish a new currency in which people could believe'.

By the 1930s the gold standard was deeply discredited. Economists argued that the world would never get out of the Great Depression if governments were limited to having only the amount of paper money that was backed by physical gold holdings. The gold standard had worked from 1819 until 1914, mainly because of the rash of gold discoveries; gold from Australia, New Zealand, South Africa and North America (including the Klondike rush in 1896) provided enough new gold to allow the printing of more money as credit and industry expanded economies. The world has changed since then, and 3,000 tonnes of gold a year from the world's mines would be grossly inadequate for such a role today.

One of the lesser-known gold standard episodes involved Japan. The economy had been weakened severely by trade deficits that persisted through the 1920s. Then the Hamaguchi government made a dreadful decision: as of January 1930, the country was placed back on the gold standard. Japan was faced with twin shocks — the spread around the world of the Great Depression and the sudden appreciation of the now gold-backed yen. Two months after the gold standard had been reintroduced, *The Economist* was able to report the consequences: in the first thirty days after the gold standard was reintroduced, the Bank of Japan saw a huge outflow of the yellow metal from its reserves and, because paper money had to be backed by those reserves, there was a sudden contraction in the amount of money in circulation, the very opposite of what was needed to keep the economy on an even keel. The magazine noted that 'the numbers out of work have risen sharply and the move for wage reductions has seriously set in. Trade disputes have naturally arisen in great numbers'.

Panicked, the government in December 1931 brought back as finance minister the former prime minister Korekiyo Takahashi. He ended the gold standard on his first day back in power. (Five years later, that same financial insight had dreadful consequences for him. After the economy began growing again, Takahashi decided to reduce government spending in order to avoid the ravages of inflation. That included curbing military budgets. The end result was that on 26 February 1936, a group of ultra-nationalist army officers assassinated the 81-year-old Takahashi in front of his wife, shooting him seven times and slashing him with a sword.)

In 1981 the then deputy head of the National Bank of Hungary, Janos Fekete, said this at an international monetary conference: 'There are about 300 economists who are against gold — and they might be right. Unfortunately, there are about three billion inhabitants of the world who still believe in it'. That comment was included in an article in *Time* magazine dated 22 June 1981, which carried the headline 'The Legacy of King Croesus'. The article was all about the increasing discussion at the time as to whether it was time to revisit going back to the gold standard.

A year earlier, *Time* had reported a group of conservative economists had been lobbying the then new Reagan administration to go back to the gold standard — not a crazy thought seeing it had been only ten years since President Richard Nixon had cut the link between the metal and the greenback. It is an idea that always seems to pop up in times of economic crisis.

And one of Benito Mussolini's earliest ideas when he seized power in Italy was to link the lira to gold in order to kill the lira's even-then joke currency status. He had King Victor Emmanuel III decree that the central bank of Italy must limit the amount of liras in circulation so there was always a forty per cent gold cover for the notes in circulation. It was a disaster because Italy suddenly did not have enough money to pay its import bills. The gold standard was quickly abandoned.

4.

IT'S ALL ABOUT THE FUNDAMENTALS

FUNDAMENTAL # 1: CAN WE GUARANTEE GOLD SUPPLY?

IN 2015 GOLDMAN SACHS began talking about 'peak gold'. One hesitates to think there might be something in this (unlike all the other 'peak' scenarios). In 1930, as mentioned previously, the gold delegation at the League of Nations warned member countries that by 1940 production of the metal would slump seriously. This report was used as an argument for further phasing out gold's role in currencies, and that gold should not be the be-all and end-all of a nation's reserves position. The year that report was produced saw world gold production at 648 tons. By 1936 the output had reached 1,030 tons. In 1940, far from slumping, the world's gold mines churned out 1,310 tons of the metal. The overall total did not fall below the 1,000-ton mark until 1943, but that occurred only because Franklin D. Roosevelt put pressure on the British Empire to slow gold output and, instead, supply metals more important for manufacturing war materiel (and he ordered U.S. gold mines closed, into the bargain).

This writer has long been sceptical about price forecasts. But analyst Eugene King at Goldman Sachs was in 2015 not drawing up imaginary price scenarios; rather he was looking at the trend of discoveries. And he is not the first to be alarmed by what those figures show. For example, the gold price in 2008 was still rising. The metal had begun that year at $835/oz, enough to whet the appetite of any gold explorer, and it kept climbing to near $1,900/oz by 2011. Yet gold discoveries did not buck up — and, remember, the gold boom was by 2008 in its seventh year, so the mining industry had lifted its exploration game considerably. In fact, discoveries had reached their zenith in 1995, a year that saw gold not quite able to breach the $400/oz level; that year, 140 million ounces of mineable gold were found. In 2013, a year that began with gold trading $1,635/oz, the discoveries totalled fewer than ten million ounces. Goldman warned that, based on the then present resource figures, the world had only twenty years of the metal left to dig out of the ground.

Of course, much more gold will be found and discoveries (and increases in resources) are still occurring. But the trend is worrying, and raises a real question as to how long the world's miners can sustain global annual production around the 3,000 tonne mark. Some say not much longer.

Let me refresh your memories of a report produced in July 2014 by U.S. consultancy, SNL Metals and Mining. It pointed out that, in the preceding twenty-four years, mining companies had discovered 1.66 billion ounces of gold (across 217 major discoveries). But while this was an impressive figure, that discovery total fell short of the 1.84 billion ounces actually mined over the same period. Taking discoveries of two million ounces or more, 124 deposits with a total 1.1 billion ounces had been found in the 1990s, but between 2000 and 2014, ninety-three discoveries had been made totalling 605 million ounces. SNL estimated that the amount of recoverable gold discovered since 1999 could eventually replace just fifty per cent of the gold produced over that same time frame.

FUNDAMENTAL # 2: IT'S ALL ABOUT CHINA

In July 2015 we saw a wave of scepticism washing over the announcement that the People's Bank of China (PBOC) had increased its official gold holdings, adding 604 tonnes since 2009, making the new total 1,658 tonnes. Bernard Dahdah, precious metals analyst at French bank Natixis put his view thus: 'It begs the question of what's been happening to the gold produced that hasn't been taken by the central bank'. One London broker said he did not believe the Chinese announcement, and wondered why Beijing was playing down its gold purchases. Another said: 'The timing (of the announcement) is as expected; it's just the amount that makes no sense'.

After all, many quite sober analysts had figured the Chinese central bank was holding somewhere between 3,000 and 4,000 tonnes; earlier in the year Bloomberg, analyzing trade data and mining production, put the country's official holdings at a quite precise 3,510 tonnes.

Just a few months earlier we heard from Alasdair Macleod, who runs the website GoldMoney. He is not your average gold bug: he has been a stockbroker since 1970, and became a member of the London Stock Exchange in 1974, and subsequently was involved with offshore banking in the Channel Islands. In early 2015 he said his conclusion was that the Chinese state owned between 25,000 and 30,000 tonnes of gold — which, even at the lower figure, would have given Beijing reserves greater than the other seventeen largest reserves holders put together, including the U.S., the International Monetary Fund, the European Central Bank, France, Italy and Germany.

His case was that China had been at it quietly since 1983 (when gold ownership in China was liberalized) through to 2002 (when the Shanghai Gold Exchange was formed). The 1983 date coincides with start of a Western bear market in gold, when repositories were sold off over a fifteen-year period. Macleod's view was that it was not just about China: all the other members of the Shanghai Cooperation Organization (Tajikistan, Kazakhstan, Kyrgyzstan, Uzbekistan, India, Iran, Pakistan and Mongolia) were in 2015 gold-friendly and/or had increased their gold reserves. 'So the West, having ditched gold for its own paper, will now find that gold has a new role as Asia's ultimate money for over three billion people,' he concluded. There is evidence that China's gold policies are not just a recent phenomenon.

We have been reading for years about the amounts of gold imported by China. In 2013, for example, China mined 437 tonnes and imported 1,033 tonnes. And that pattern of increasing mine output and a steady import flow has been repeated over six years. In the first three months of 2015, Chinese mines lifted output by fourteen per cent and refined 110.7 tonnes. In 2014, the Swiss sent 600 tonnes to China. In 2013, one month — July — saw 106.4 tonnes move from Hong Kong into China. In November 2014 Hong Kong supplies totalled 99.1 tonnes. This has gone on month after month. So, if not into the PBOC, where has that gold gone?

Sure, a good deal has gone into jewellery and bars and coins bought by private investors. And the World Gold Council estimates China's domestic banks have, since 2009, collectively added 600 tonnes of gold to their inventories.

One theory was that, if Beijing revealed its real reserves and came out with a figure closer to 3,000 tonnes, that would frighten the horses with regard to the U.S. dollar — in other words, the hair-trigger types would assume China was desperate to convert its U.S. currency holdings to something safer. China may at some stage want to deliver a blow to the greenback, but not while it still holds some $3 trillion of them. Nevertheless, the official figures on the holdings did not add up.

In 2010 a newspaper published by the Ministry of Commerce in Beijing said China should boost its gold reserves to the same level as those of the United States (then standing at 8,133 tonnes). At that time, too, Erste Bank of Austria cited another Chinese official who had recently called for reserves of 10,000 tonnes by 2020 — Chinese officials don't make these sorts of comments off the cuff and without approval — which the Austrian bank said would involve China buying forty per cent of global mine production over the next following years.

Richard Russell, the veteran U.S. newsletter writer who published *The Dow Theory Letters* since 1958, at the time posed these questions: 'Why is China now the world's leading miner of gold? Why is China literally begging its people to buy and hoard gold? Why has China opened new gold trading facilities? Why is China installing dispensing machines in public places so that people can insert their paper money and buy small quantities of gold? Why is it forbidden to ship or carry gold out of China?'

David Hale, the widely quoted Chicago-based economist, may have provided the answer in an October 2010 article. Arguing that China was the key to the gold price, he pointed out an interesting historical precedent for what he believed we might be about to see. In 1913, the United States held 2,293 tonnes of gold against Britain's 248 tonnes. 'The Americans' large gold reserves made the dollar a natural replacement for sterling when the First World War crippled Britain's financial position,' he wrote. By 2010 the U.S. was running the same fiscal policy as Britain had in the 1940s — that is, going into debt — as London was forced to do to finance the war.

Washington saw gold as a way to project financial power, and China probably sees it the same way now, Hale argued.

In just thirty years, China has gone from being a minor producer to the world's largest source of mined gold. The news coverage of the World Gold Council's early 2015 report on China's gold market had — quite rightly — concentrated on the outlook for sales and its implications for the metal's trading price. But the report also had some fascinating detail on the transformation of the gold sector in China since the 1949 revolution. The changes hinge on the 1978 economic and market reforms undertaken by Beijing. Until then, gold production in China had been less than ten tonnes a year. In 1950, after Mao Tse-tung's Communist Party established its authority over all of mainland China, gold bullion ownership was prohibited and what little gold mining there was (along with everything else in China) came under state control.

But China never lost its appetite for the yellow metal. In the 1960s, the *Christian Science Monitor* newspaper took very seriously the words of Franz Pick, then the New York-based doyen of the gold bug movement. A refugee from the Austro-Hungarian Empire, the ageing pundit published

Pick's World Currency Report and also what he called an advance obituary for the U.S. dollar. One pronouncement of Pick's got a very big run in the *Monitor* in 1966.

'When an addict in Harlem buys his drugs, he may well be directly providing Communist China with gold,' the report began. Pick was just repeating charges made before the United Nations Commission on Narcotic Drugs. It was said some 2,000 tonnes a year of opium and morphine were produced in Yunnan, then shipped to the West through Laos and the Portuguese colony of Macau. Pick argued that the payments for these drugs had enabled China to buy sizeable quantities of gold. Indeed, the Bank of International Settlements estimated China's 1965 gold purchases as being worth $150 million (that year gold averaged $35.15/oz).

In a subsequent report, the *Monitor* again quoted Pick, this time saying that China was also raising money for gold purchases through war-torn Vietnam. The Viet Cong, the insurgents serving communist North Vietnam in the civil war against the U.S.-backed South Vietnam, had infiltrated the south and controlled most of the currency black market, through which most American servicemen changed their dollars into South Vietnamese piasters. These dollars were sent to Hong Kong where the communist controlled Bank of China changed them into sterling, which was then used to buy gold through the London market.

China was buying gold because it could not produce enough of its own. But after 1978, when the destructive policies of the Cultural Revolution were finally ditched, the Chinese government turned its attention to (among other things) boosting gold production. The People's Liberation Army set up a special gold mining unit whose goal was to prospect for gold and develop mines. This move, along with liberalization, meant that China's gold production by the early 1990s was running at more than 100 tonnes a year. Then between 1994 and 2013 production surged by more than 300 tonnes a year. Between 1994 and 2013, China's share of world mine output rose from nine per cent to nearly fifteen per cent.

The shape of the gold industry changed, too. Today about half the gold mined in China comes from the top ten producers, the remainder from the more than 600 mines. In 2010 China moved decisively to do something about its National Gold Group Corporation, a state-owned enterprise with its headquarters in Beijing and which controls about twenty per cent of the country's gold output; that year the corporation did a deal to acquire half the output of the new Kensington gold mine in Alaska operated by Coeur d'Alene Mines. The mine was expected to average 125,000oz a year.

That year also saw China Railway Engineering Corp buy a majority stake in a project to develop the vast Las Cristinas gold deposit in Venezuela's southern jungles in partnership with Canada's Crystallex International. The deposit had an estimated seventeen million ounces of gold. Here's the interesting aspect: the Canadians had held the project for several years but had not been able to clear permission to mine after a dispute with the Chavez government. The Chinese apparently saw themselves as being able to unblock the permitting process. It is not just unlimited amounts of money available to these Chinese corporations, they can use their political leverage in treacherous jurisdictions to give them bargaining power over mining rights.

In 2010 the official *China Daily* reported that Shandong Gold Mining Group planned 'to expand its bullion output and also grow inorganically through overseas acquisitions'. The company was seeking to increase its output by up to thirty tonnes over the next year to meet domestic demand for gold. South America, Canada and Australia were mentioned in the report as places where Shandong would be looking.

At that time, too, John R. Ing of Maison Placement Canada, a research firm and investment bank, shared his view of the Chinese gold industry: 'There are over 1,500 miners or so of the mom-and-pop variety,' he said. 'Chinese mines are actually a whole bunch of small and shallow gold mines with short reserve lives. Chinese miners are more interested in cash flow rather than spending money to extend reserves.' Ing said that, down the road, China would need to boost its reserves and acquire Western technology, software and underground expertise. He made the point that, while China was by then the largest gold producer in the world, it could be a very short-lived number one position, with China's gold status being highly vulnerable.

Remember the case of South Africa, he warned —the country was once the number one producer but its output was now at its lowest level in 100 years.

This push abroad by Chinese gold miners stems from the fact that, as the World Gold Council believes, there are doubts China's present production levels can be maintained. Indeed, these could peak in the next few years due to declining reserve base, falling grades and consequent rising production costs.

Just look at what happened in the country's number one gold producing area, Zhaoyuan County in Shandong province. By 2013 its golden days appear numbered: the city had sixty-eight gold mines but local authorities were concerned many of these would be exhausted within fifteen years, partly due to the cranking up of output to meet domestic demand for gold. The mines in Zhaoyuan have dropped their actual extraction average from 4 grams per tonne to two grams, while costs are rising (by about eight per cent in 2012) due to more expensive equipment, power and labour.

The U.S. Geological Survey has estimated remaining Chinese gold reserves at 1,900 tonnes, out of a world total of 52,000 tonnes. The country is now producing fifteen per cent of the world's gold but has only four per cent of the known reserves. As the WGC notes, the rest of the world's reserves will, based on 2013 output, last an average 19.7 years, China's at the present rate of extraction will last only 4.3 years. 'Anecdotal evidence is that exploration success in China, as in many parts of the world, has been conspicuous in its absence in the past decade,' the WGC report says.

Reuters was reporting in early 2015 that Chinese gold output was set to slow considerably. Quoting Business Monitor International, *Reuters* was reporting declining ore grades, depleting reserves and waning profitability that, taken together, meant China would have to raise its imports of gold 'to meet the persistent strength in demand from Chinese consumers'.

But the gold council did not think China would run out of gold quite as quickly as the raw numbers suggest. This was because China claims a larger reserve total than presented by the U.S.G.S. — China's reserve figure is 6,000 tonnes according to the Ministry of Land and Resources, or between 15,000 tonnes and 20,000 tonnes according to the China Geological and

Mineral Survey (which tells you something about Chinese figures, if nothing else).

Regardless of that, there seems little doubt grades are falling and costs are rising faster than inflation in China. The WGC believes that the 2013 gold price retreat after the heady period in 2011-12 will have resulted in plummeting cash margins in China, making many smaller mines loss-makers and accelerating closures and shortening mine lives.

❦

This Chinese interest (many would say obsession) with gold is no recent development.

In 1980, the *Los Angeles Times* correspondent in China reported that 'a gold rush is on in China', the metal's price then ranging between $600/oz and $700/oz. It would go higher but, as we know, the excitement did not last long. At that time, though, the Chinese authorities were seeing gold as one revenue source for their modernization plan. Peking (as it then was) encouraged peasants to go prospecting to find new deposits.

In 1982 Chinese were allowed to buy gold jewellery. Then panda-bearing gold coins were issued in four weights. Even after the price plunged, China backed gold production. In 1985 it sought to encourage more exploration (and deter smuggling of gold abroad) by raising the official price paid from $175 to $250.

Nor is there any doubting of Chinese interest in gold. In 1988 the *Washington Post* reported that Qinghai province was experiencing the country's greatest ever scramble for gold. Over two years, it was estimated that forty prospectors had been killed in gun battles over ground. In 1989 the *Christian Science Monitor* said an estimated 400,000 peasants had abandoned their land to look for gold.

There are sporadic news reports that Chinese gold buying (mainly in the form of jewellery) has plunged. But to consider this the end of the Chinese gold buying spree is delusional. The Chinese have not lost interest in (or their taste for) the yellow metal. They are just biding their time, or are temporarily diverted by bubbles (the one in early 2015 being the meteoric rise of share prices on the Shanghai Stock Exchange).

The problem is that many Western observers are not distinguishing between the present (concentrating on just the price) and the long term (which is all about ownership of the world's gold).

On one U.S. website, there appeared in early 2015 a translation of a piece purportedly appearing on the *Sina* news service. *Sina* is based in Shanghai, was founded in 1999, and runs a Chinese-language news service for Chinese abroad. This item was said to be an opinion piece written for *Sina* by Song Xin, president of the China Gold Association. He was advocating that China (presumably meaning the Chinese central bank) should accumulate 8,500 tonnes of gold (adding: 'more than the U.S.'). Song said China would not *back* the yuan with gold, but *support* it with gold 'so it has sufficient credibility for the world to accept it as a trade and reserve currency'.

What is perhaps astonishing in light of these trends is that the great preponderance of gold coverage in Western media is preoccupied with what happens in New York and in the exchange-traded funds, and gold v. the dollar. The ETFs are increasingly becoming a sideshow.

FUNDAMENTAL # 3: GOLD MINERS HAVE TO MAKE A PROFIT FOR THEIR SHAREHOLDERS

In 1999 there was a real fear that the gold industry was in peril. There were reports that miners in many gold-producing countries were being laid off. On 7 July, *Time* magazine reported that 'next they'll be having an "everything must go" sale at Fort Knox'. The Bank of England had just sold twenty-five tonnes, sending the gold price even lower, and there were grave fears the International Monetary Fund would starting selling off as much as $2.6 billion of its gold reserves in order to finance debt relief to poor countries.

It is hard to make a profit from mining gold at those 1999 levels, when the metal got below $260/oz.. But, for all the wonder of the gold rise between 2002 and 2011, shareholders did not see all that much of the benefits, especially from the smaller mining companies. It was one of the black spots of the great gold boom that all too rarely did this translate into dividends, and it was a feature of many years that gold shares did not keep pace with the rise in the metal's price.

It is possible to pay the type of dividends that will have investors rushing to buy your stock. If you were a shareholder in the gold miner Colorado Dredging Company in 1913 you did very well out of mining the yellow metal. That year the company paid a dividend of $2.50 a share, so for 1,000 shares you would have received a cheque (or check) for $2,500. In 2015 terms, that would be equivalent to $65,227 (according to the American Institute for Economic Research's cost of living calculator).

No wonder people could live off their investments in those days. This was not a lone example. In 1923, a gold dredging company announced a dividend of 60c a share. That would be $8.29 in 2015 money. But, back then, that dividend for 1,000 shares would total $600, when an average car cost $265. The payment for forty-five shares would be enough to pay for a Wilton rug. The payout for one share would have bought you a dozen eggs, or 2.5 kilograms of flour or a dozen oranges.

Also, in 1923 Consolidated Gold Fields of South Africa paid a dividend of three shillings a share, meaning that if you owned 1,000 shares there would be a cheque of £150. In today's purchasing power, that is equivalent to £7,460.

If you own stock in a gold mining company, you can easily do the comparison: how much would the dividend from one share buy you? Certainly not a dozen eggs, perhaps not even one egg.

Part of reason for the high dividends back then was that companies obviously took the view that the money earned by the company belonged to shareholders (and their labour costs were low). Therefore, what was available was given to those very shareholders. Thus in 1928 Consolidated Gold Fields made a profit of £736,000. It put £100,000 into reserves, held

£52,400 for working expenses, then paid out all the remainder in dividends. In 1934, during the Great Depression, Wiluna Gold Corporation paid a dividend equivalent to 22.5 per cent of the face value of its one pound shares.

5.

GOLD BOOMS – AND BUSTS

W HAT HAS BEEN MISSING for nigh on thirty-five years is a
good, old-fashioned gold panic. Like this example of a headline in
the *Los Angeles Times* of 4 January 1980: 'Up, Up, Up: Gold soars to $649 in
near panic pace'. The opening paragraph stated: 'Gold prices spiralled upwards at a near-panic pace Thursday as buyers, worried by the international
crises in Iran and Afghanistan, drove the price per ounce of the precious
metal on all major world markets to levels more than $100 higher than
just two days ago'. Gold was selling at $649.73/oz in Hong Kong when the
paper went to press. Apart from the eerie parallels with those same trouble spots today, that two-day climb represented would, if the percentage
was replicated today, see gold rise by around $310/oz over two sessions.
Wouldn't that be something?

Another headline: from the *Chicago Tribune* of 1 March 1983, this
blasted across the page: 'Gold plunges 10% in wave of panic selling'. The
report opens that 'Waves of panic selling, stemming from fears that falling
oil prices would lead to worldwide deflation, drove prices of gold and other
precious metals down sharply on Monday in bullion markets around the
globe'.

Could investors cope with those sort of single-session moves today? In
fact, going thirty-five years without a severe gold panic is unusual. They

came thick and fast for much of the twentieth century — so why couldn't another be around the corner?

Take a look at 1931: then there was real panic about whether paper money could be trusted; many people still wanted the surety of gold. As *Time* magazine reported, 'Chileans learned, not without grief, that half of the Central Bank of Chile's gold reserve is in British pounds — i.e. has turned to paper. Even Paris, where lies twenty per cent of the world's banking gold was uneasy, extra prudent". (No, there's not a word missing: that was how *Time* used to be written.) The cause: from Britain to Colombo to Uruguay, paper money was no longer tied to gold. Colombia banned the export of gold.

Fast-forward to 1937. The six members of the Gold Committee — the chaps who set the London gold fix each morning at 11am — were on one day faced with sell orders totalling 1,493 bars of the metal, or $21 million worth (quite a tidy sum for 1937). This followed rumours that the U.S. was going to cut its gold buying price. That week, $65 million worth of gold passed through Rothschild's trading desk alone. Most of the gold was bought by the Bank of England to help end the panic.

In October 1960 — what is it about October that brings on market panics? — London's *Daily Express* (then a middlebrow broadsheet) headlined its front page with the words 'Gold fever!'. On London's then eight-year-old gold exchange, prices rose 16.3 per cent. But in Hong Kong, gold soared thirty-two per cent that day. It was set off by bad economic news from the U.S. and investors seeking to sell their greenbacks in favour of gold.

Just imagine what the reaction would be today if gold rose 16.3 per cent in one sitting.

6.

HOW HARD IS IT
TO FIND GOLD?

Major gold discoveries in the twenty-first century

2001	6
2002	7
2003	13
2004	9
2005	13
2006	19
2007	14
2008	9
2009	10
2010	6
2011	4
2012	3
2013	4
2014	2
2015	2
2016	2
2017	0

Source: S&P Global Market Intelligence

THE GOLD PRICE IS not necessarily a guide to the pace of the hunt for gold. In fact, over the past few decades, more gold has been discovered when the metal's value was in the basement than when it was soaring. In other words, gold was easier to find in the 1990s (when the miners were moving out of their well-explored home territories, into various parts of the developing world). What should be a concern now is that, with mining companies active in multiple jurisdictions, gold is simply getting harder to find on a worldwide basis.

In 1998, when the gold price averaged $294.16/oz, the world saw fifteen major gold discoveries. By contrast, as shown in statistics compiled by S&P Global Market Intelligence, in 2012 when gold averaged $1,669.82/oz, only three major gold discoveries were made around the globe. In 2014, 2015 and 2016, only two such discoveries were recorded in each of those years. And in 2017? None.

S&P also found, in its 2018 study of gold discoveries, that spending on gold exploration in 2017 remained at historically high levels. Between 1990 and 2008, $32.2 billion was spend trying to discover gold (with 222 significant discoveries). But in the years since, that has increased to $54.3 billion (but yielding only forty-one such discoveries).

This be may be a chicken-and-egg situation: mining companies are now focusing more on expanding existing mine resources or expanding new discoveries by nearby drilling. Is this because new discoveries are now so hard to find, or are their fewer discoveries in greenfield areas because the miners are preferring to stick close to existing ones rather than take on new gambles?

Furthermore, if you are a cashed-up gold producer, then how much easier it is to acquire another producer or an operating project.

And when gold is found it takes a while before the first pour. The World Bank says the average is 10 years between those two events; another source says thirteen years. And according to a paper by Richard Schodde of Melbourne-based MinEx Consulting there have been 1,992 significant gold discoveries around the world since 1950. But only 1,018 of those were developed into mines — a fifty-one per cent success rate.

There has been on and off talk over the past few years of 'peak gold'. In 2015 Goldman Sachs estimated that known reserves would last for only another twenty years. In 2017 Randall Oliphant, chairman of the World Gold Council, wondered aloud whether global gold production had reached its peak.

In 2016 Nick Holland of Gold Fields warned that the industry was not spending enough to sustain itself into the future (even though, as we know, gold exploration has taken the lion's share of world exploration spending of late). Holland made the comments after studying eleven leading gold companies and discovering that all of them were facing reduced mine life futures. (In 2016, gold miner Petropavlovsk cut its exploration budget by two-thirds.)

The post-2013 fall in the gold price also encourage miners to focus on higher-grade areas, leaving the lower grades for later, so burning up their reserves.

As the Minerals Council of Australia has explained, gold discoveries in that country are being found at increasing depth (and witness, too, the decision to extend the Gwalia mine to a depth of 2km). "Since the 1950s, the average depth for greenfield discoveries has increased from zero to forty-three metres," the MCA notes. The average depth for brownfield discoveries has increased from twenty to 110 metres. This both increases the cost of mining and lengthens the development time frame.

But, wait, there's more from the MCA: 'Whereas the average size of gold discoveries was 2.2 million ounces between 1980 and 1989, it was half that at just 1.1 million ounces from 2000 to 2009. The average grade of discoveries similarly halved over the decade'. Moreover, as well as the size, the average *grade* of discoveries also halved over the decade, in part reflecting changing styles of mineralisation that comprise the bulk of gold exploration targets. 'This includes porphyry style deposits where gold occurs in combination with other metals, principally copper and, to a lesser extent, silver and molybdenum. These deposits often require more costly and complex processing', the council noted.

In late 2017 Pierre Lassonde, who co-founded Franco-Nevada, told the German financial newspaper *Finanz und Wirtschaft* that for the past 130 years all of the world's known massive gold deposits had been mined and many worked out. Eventually legendary gold fields such as the Witwatersrand Basin, the Carlin Trend and the Super Pit would become things of the past, he added.

Deposits with at least five million ounces in reserves are the types of mines that now produce around half the world's gold; as more of these large deposits become exhausted, the world's gold supply needs are going to depend heavily on a rising number of smaller operations.

***

Then there is the China factor. Back in February 2017 the Chinese news agency Xinhua reported that 150 of China's 600-odd gold mines were being closed down. Since then we have read other reports about the shuttering of 'antiquated' mines, and that many are going out of business because of 'low' gold prices. In fact one report from China described the mines being closed as 'outdated production capacity'.

So China has decided to leave gold in the ground because they can't afford to mine it at $1,200/oz (with Chinese wage levels)? This strained one's credulity. If they are closing mines, then it is more likely to be because deposits are being exhausted. This, if my hunch is right, tells us that China's gold industry is having a spot of trouble. It also bodes well for anyone with an economic gold project or mine because Chinese appetites for gold appear unabated.

Figures out of Beijing showed that Chinese gold mine output in the first quarter of 2017 fell 9.3 per cent year on year, from 111.5 tonnes to 101.2 tonnes, presumably brought about as mines were closing down. Yet at that same time, while interest in the metal on a global scale waned, Chinese investor buying was up thirty per cent year on year (gold bars up sixty per cent). The Hong Kong stock exchange was, also at the same time, launching a new gold futures contract priced in yuan.

It has been long assumed that, given China's insatiable appetite for the metal, the country would have to raise its imports of gold to meet the persistent strength in demand from Chinese consumers. But the very strong preference is for Chinese companies to control the source of those imports.

More and more of the gold being produced is going to end up in Chinese hands. This is going to put even greater pressure on Western miners to find new sources of gold to satisfy other demand.

At present rates of extraction, the next thirty years should see a further 97,000 tonnes of gold pulled from the Earth. But as Mark Fellows, head of mine supply at London-based precious metals consultancy Metals Focus explains, at the end of 2016 the globe's known remaining gold reserves totalled just over 55,000 tonnes. He adds that, even by allowing a generous metallurgical recovery factory of ninety per cent, this would allow the industry with only fifteen years of production at the present rate of extraction.

However, Metals Focus estimates that another 110,000 tonnes can be proven up — enough to carry the world through to 2048. But Fellows has a caveat: 'This gold mineralisation cannot be classified as reserves because its recovery is either uneconomic at current prices or it has not received the detailed study required to prove its profitable recovery'.

But back to that reserves figure of 55,000 tonnes: production costs have risen by about ten per cent a year for the previous fifteen years, so Metals Focus estimates that a gold price of around $1,500/oz is required to maintain gold output at its current levels. This assumes an average $75/oz discovery cost, average capital cost of $200/oz, all-in sustaining costs not going above $1,150/oz and leaving a fifteen per cent return on investment.

For all the geographical expansion of gold operations, Canada and Australia between them still account for thirty-three per cent of spending on gold exploration, with another nine per cent being spent in the U.S. In 2017 Africa, in spite of its size and prospectivity, saw just fifteen per cent of exploration budgets. And Russia? Only three per cent.

POSTSCRIPT

I F YOU WANT CONSPIRACY theories, gold's your boy. The big favourite is that 'they' — meaning the central banks hand-in-hand with major financial institutions — have been artificially repressing the gold price for years. As with all good conspiracy theories, the case has a certain plausibility. But another theme running through much of the online discussion about gold in recent years involved the actions of President Franklin D Roosevelt in 1933, when the United States government made illegal the private ownership of gold.

Could a government do that again?

You have to look at the context. As banks collapsed in the Great Depression, Americans rushed to exchange their paper money for gold (the yellow metal then backed the dollar) but, of course, there simply wasn't enough gold in the vaults to cover all the paper notes in circulation.

Moreover, the U.S. suffered serious gold drains to foreign countries — those foreigners wanted to take their assets home as a hard asset, not as a promissory note from Washington. So, in addition to private ownership, Washington also banned the exporting of gold. It would not be until 1974 that President Gerald Ford reinstated the right of private gold ownership to American citizens.

But I think (and hope) we can rest easy about gold and government seizures. In 1933, relatively few people around the world owned gold; now gold ownership is rising in China, Australia, Europe and the Middle East. It is a totally different ball game.

However, we live in uncertain times, so it might be instructive to examine what really did happen in 1933. An article written soon after the event

('Gold, Banks and the New Deal', by James W. Angell, in the *Political Science Quarterly*, December 1934) explains that the abandonment of the gold standard and the subsequent ban on private ownership or export of gold 'must be viewed as part of a general program of currency and credit inflation then being developed'.

The Roosevelt move was very much of its time and provoked by specific financial considerations that do not apply today. At the time, the U.S. held about a quarter of the monetary gold in the world and in 1933 its stockpile was worth $2.7 billion. No, what it was about was adjusting the value of the dollar to between fifty per cent and sixty percent of the former gold value. Roosevelt faced a situation where banks were failing, the silver industry was trying to get its metal remonetized and the U.S. financial system was verging on collapse.

As Angell argues, 'on the very day of the inauguration itself (4 March 1933), President Roosevelt found an unprecedented economic crisis confronting him. The banking system of the entire country had collapsed almost overnight; industry and trade had fallen to new depths; and a severe national emergency had developed'. By this stage, the United States had the worst record in the world for bank failures. In 1921 there had been 30,800 banks across the country; at the end of 1933, there were 15,200 remaining —that is more than half the banks gone in a space of twelve years. In 1931 2,298 banks collapsed, taking with them deposits of $1.69 billion. In 1933 another 1,780 banks closed their doors. In fact, over the period 1930 to 1933, more than 10,000 banks went out of business.

This in turn created more panic, and gold flowed out of the country. What is more, the United States had been on the gold standard; the nationalization of gold was in step with America leaving the gold standard.

Economic historians have, over the past decade, not treated Roosevelt well, many arguing persuasively that much of his New Deal and many of his financial regulations made matters worse and triggered a second collapse in 1937. But it is not that complex issue which is remembered today. What remains is that Roosevelt was seen as a virtual dictator — in fact, newspaper headlines used that very term. When the deadline for the handing in of all gold expired on 27 March 1933, the Federal Reserve had taken possession of metal worth $503 million. But then, as *The New York Times* reported the next day, Roosevelt had previously ordered a list to be drawn up of all those who had, in the previous two years, drawn out large sums of gold and had not returned it. It left as very nasty taste — and one that still resonates today.

But, this time it is different. True, the financial system is shaky. But we can probably put to bed the fear that we'll see any western government seize gold because, unlike 1933, there is no longer the gold standard that caused the problem in the first place. Hoard away.

APPENDIX 1:
GOLD AS A FINANCIAL INSTRUMENT

L OOK AT THE CHANGE in end uses for gold in the space of a mere ten years. In 2001, 3,009 tonnes went into jewellery and 357 tonnes into investment (bars and coins, etc.) Half way through that decade, the balance had already tipped a great deal the other way: in 2006, 2,298 tonnes went into jewellery and 676 tonnes into investment – this latter figure not quite doubling in five years but getting pretty close. And by 2011 they were almost level pegging: 1,963 tonnes into jewellery and 1,641 tonnes into investment. In the case of the latter, in ten years the investment demand for gold had grown more than four-fold.

And that was in spite of it being so much more expensive to invest in the yellow metal. In 2001, gold averaged $270 an ounce, in 2006 $638/oz and in 2011 $1,567/oz. So, it seems that jewellery demand may have slackened off because of the price, but investment did not.

For all this, global gold production did not increase in line with investment growth (from 2,600 tonnes in 2001 to 2,821 tonnes in 2011).

Also changing was the country-by-country policies of central bank buying of gold. The biggest seller between 2001 and 2011 was Switzerland, followed by France, the International Monetary Fund, the Netherlands, the

United Kingdom and the European Central Bank. All firmly in the developed world.

The biggest accumulators were China (even though, no doubt, the quantity was vastly under-reported), followed by Russia, the Bank of International Settlements, India, Saudi Arabia, Singapore and Mexico — mainly players from emerging markets, the BIS excepted. (Some eighty-eight countries, including Canada, have no gold reserves. Norway is the only European country without gold reserves.)

Russia is at present one of the big buyers, accumulating another 300,000 ounces in March 2018. Russia also keeps all its gold reserves within its own borders. And here we have another trend: governments increasingly distrust others to look after their gold.

After war broke out in 1939, huge gold shipments were sent to the United States for safety. The U.S., Britain and France have long been used to store gold. But, more and more, governments are these days moving their bullion back home. We saw Germany pull gold out of U.S. vaults (half its reserves) and more recently Hungary moved all its gold back to Budapest.

Turkey set out in 2018 to do the same, but that is being seen more as a political slap in the face to America than a risk decision. However, booming inflation and sinking currency saw demand for gold surge in Turkey in 2018 as people sought to protect their wealth. The Turks spent $965 million in the three months to March 31 on gold, up thirty-four per cent on the same period in 2017.Furthermore, Turkey's central bank has been an aggressive gold buyer from early 2017, almost doubling its holdings within twelve months.

All the above feeds into a report out from the World Gold Council (WGC) arguing that gold can be used to hedge emerging market risk. It points out that economic growth is a key driver of gold demand, especially in emerging market countries where there is a high affinity for gold as jewellery and investment. At present seventy per cent of gold demand come from emerging market countries.

The WGC produces a map showing gold demand as a ten-year average to December 2017. The United States and Canada accounted for ten per cent; Europe and Russia twelve per cent. But China, over those ten years, accounted for twenty-four per cent of demand, India and Pakistan another twenty-four per cent, the Middle East twelve per cent and Southeast Asia eight per cent.

The council's argument is that a U.S. investor holding emerging market securities always has as their greatest worry any unexpected currency movements. The council said its research shows that emerging market portfolios that included an allocation to gold generally outperformed portfolios without gold. Over ten years to 2017, gold may not have matched U.S. stocks or emerging market stocks for performance (which are the usual comparisons) but the yellow metal handily beat U.S. cash, U.S. bonds, the EAFE (Europe, Australasia and Far East) index and thrashed commodity price performance. Over a twenty-year period only U.S. stocks put in a better performance than gold.

Every so often we hear talk of gold being irrelevant. No, it is still, in fact, misunderstood and keeps evolving in terms of investment sophistication.

Appendix 2:
Silver, the poor relation

Top producing countries (2016, millions of ounces)

Mexico   186.2

Peru   147.7

China   112.4

Chile   48.1

Russia4   6.6

Australia   43.6

Bolivia   43.5

Poland   38.5

United States   35.4

Argentina   30.0

Top silver producing companies (2016, millions of ounces)

Fresnillo   45.7

Glencore   39.1

KGHM Polska Miedz 38.8

Polymetal Int.   29.2

Goldcorp   28.1

Pan American Silver   25.3

Top producing primary silver mines (2016, millions of ounces)
Saucito, Mexico   21.9

Escobel, Guatemala   21.2

Dukat, Russia   19.8

Cannington, Australia 18.2

Uchucchacua, Peru   16.2

Fresnillo, Mexico   15.0

Source: Silver Institute

CRITICAL METAL, TECHNOLOGY METAL and precious metal all wrapped into one and (as of when this was being written) all yours for the modest price of around $16.50 an ounce. Silver is one of the more fascinating technology metals, cheap and plentiful. Silver demand is rising from sectors involved in security, health care, clean energy and water purification.

However, that is a two-edged sword: now that industrial uses account for more than fifty per cent of silver use, it is in danger of being increasingly classified as an industrial metal, and losing its aura of being a precious metal. For a while, a few years ago, it was neatly balanced; that is, you could sell the line that silver was unique is being considered equally an industrial and a precious metal.

But, by 2018, sentiment was beginning to shift — against silver's role as a precious metal.

Apparently, at least fourteen languages use the same word for silver as for money — French (*argent*), Welsh (*arian*) and Swahili (*fedha*) among them. Silver has been coined as money since 700 BC, although it was separated from lead as early as 4000 BC. It has been a hard row to hoe in recent years arguing silver's continuing role as money (unlike gold, where the case 'for' is close to conclusive). The languishing price and the gold:silver ratio illustrate the uphill task. At one stage, just a few years ago, it was possible to argue that silver had a unique appeal: it was both (and almost equally so) both a precious metal and an industrial one.

Silver has suffered in modern times due to its image as gold's 'poor relation'. Back in 1883, an ounce of gold was sixteen times more valuable than an ounce of silver. By, 1900, the ratio was 32:1. It reached its greatest disparity in 1991 when the ratio was 93:1, and it seemed that anyone who talked about mining silver was ignored — if not laughed at.

The problem with silver — and the problem for silver investors — was that for several years the metal could not make up its mind which one it was: a store of value or an industrial metal. In fact, it was both — which made it hard to value. With gold or copper, you know where you stand. Gold is primarily a store of value, some say the only real form of currency (although plenty have argued in the past that silver should be included in that definition). Gold's price rises with political risk, falls with political peace, rises with the debasement of fiat currencies, and falls when investors flee to the U.S. dollar when that currency is seen as a safe haven. With copper, though, price stands or falls on industrial demand (or Chinese import demand).

However, the scales have become more heavily weighted to the industrial side due, on one hand, to the abovementioned doubts about silver's value as a precious metal (outside the ranks of millions of American silver coin hoarders) and, on the other, to the several emerging industrial roles for the white metal.

Investors may these days swoon over graphite, lithium and cobalt, but silver is a rich —pardon the expression — part of the world's mining heritage. After 5,000 years, silver's story and development are far from standing still.

As the Washington-based Silver Institute reminds us, the white metal was first mined in about 3000 BC in what is now Turkey. By 1000 AD, Spain was the leader in silver production, mines in that country being the principal suppliers for the Roman Empire. Silver was the instrument of trade. But, once the Moors invaded the Iberian peninsula, Europeans had to get their silver elsewhere and, by 1500 AD, this led to many mines being opened to meet the growing demand for the metal.

But then came the discovery by Europeans of the Americas. Following the Spanish conquests, Latin America became the great source of silver; for 300 years Bolivia, Peru and Mexico between them accounted for more than eighty-five per cent of the world's output of the white metal. Centuries later came the Comstock Lode discovery in Nevada. Australia, Canada and many other countries and colonies became silver producers. In Australia's case, the island continent's first mine — apart from small coal operations that supplied the first European settlements — was a silver (and lead) one near Adelaide. It opened in 1841. Then in 1883, the lead and silver bonanza at Broken Hill was discovered, and from 1885 The Broken Hill Proprietary Company Limited was starting its extraordinary mining story on the back of silver. In 1893, silver was discovered at Mt Lyell, and another mining story was born.

But the Silver Institute points out an important inflexion point for silver: 'The period from 1876 to 1920 represented an explosion in both technological innovation and exploitation of new regions worldwide. Production over the last quarter of the 19th century quadrupled over the average of the first seventy-five years to a total of nearly 120 million troy ounces annually'. Yet since the beginning of recorded history only an estimated 1,464,700 tonnes of silver have been mined.

Silver has long and deep historical roots around the world. It was only eighty years ago that China's currency was tied to the silver standard. The 1896 presidential election in the United States was dominated by the debate over silver's role in the nation's currency (egged on by the silver mining lobby, of course). As an article published in the prestigious journal *Foreign Affairs* noted just months after the ending of the silver standard in the mid-1930s, 'few more memorable steps have been taken in monetary history'.

The journal pointed out that, for the Chinese, silver occupied what it called a 'three-tiered throne' — as a standard of value, as a medium of exchange and as a store of value. It was estimated at the time that Chinese savers had hoarded about 1.75 billion ounces of the white metal.

We have seen in India the poorer investors opt for silver because they cannot afford meaningful quantities of gold. What if the poorer Chinese follow in their footsteps?

Americans are fascinated by the metal. Thomas Jefferson had introduced the bimetallic coinage standard — that is, money being made either from gold or silver. The silver dollar was abolished in 1853, but the metal remained the standard for smaller denominations of coins. All through the latter half of the 19th century, congressmen and senators from the western silver mining states such as Idaho, Nevada and California, kept pushing for the return of bimetallism. In 1890 they succeeded in tagging one bill with a silver-purchase clause which, when passed, required the government to double its silver purchases.

The whole silver issue kept going into the twentieth century. By 1932 the metal's price was down at 35c/oz. Many Americans argued it was the fall of the silver price that caused the worst of the Great Depression, so convinced were they of the metal's importance. Western senators took to the radio waves to make eloquent pleas on behalf of silver — one tried to get a bill passed for the United States government to buy 200 million ounces and lend them to China in order to prop up that country's silver standard.

Silver surged in mid-1966, with futures contracts in New York rising in a three-month period from eight million ounces covered to almost twenty million ounces. Many in the market were expecting a big revaluation of gold, and that would pull silver up too as the white metal was pegged to the yellow one.

The United States government in 1968 set up the Silver Stockpile, run under the umbrella of the Defence National Stockpile Centre, based at Fort Belvoir, Virginia. It was established with an allocation from the U.S. Treasury of 165 million ounces of silver.

The silver rise was supported by the fact that, in 1965, global silver production was a little over 200 million ounces, but demand was hitting

700 million. The shortfall was being made up by releases of existing silver as demonetization of the metal speeded up around the world.

The most naked silver move of recent years was in 1979, when Nelson Bunker Hunt and William Herbert Hunt tried to corner the silver market and thus manipulate the price of the white metal. The brothers first came to notice in 1974 when they had accumulated contracts covering fifty-five million ounces, or eight per cent of the global supply. But they didn't flip those contracts: they wanted the physical silver delivered. They chartered three Boeing 707s to fly forty million ounces to Switzerland.

(Incidentally, they were partly motivated by a fear that President Richard Nixon — who had by then broken the gold link to the U.S .dollar — might follow the same path as one of his predecessors: back in 1933, Franklin D. Roosevelt had confiscated all private gold holdings and made people turn over the gold to the government. The Hunts thought Nixon or his successor might do the same with silver.)

By 1976 the Hunts, using the family oil money, had bought another twenty million ounces. Up and up crept the silver price as the metal's scarcity grew. They had begun buying at $4/oz; by January 1980 (helped by gold's meteoric rise as well as the Hunts' activities) it peaked at a whisker over $50/oz.

They went too far — they locked in contracts at that high price but were caught when the silver price collapsed. They then faced massive fines by U.S. regulators as well as law suits from investors. At the peak of their activity, the brothers held 400 million ounces of silver worth $15 billion.

In March 1981 it was revealed that the newly installed Reagan administration planned to sell a third of the government's silver stockpile, the $500 million in proceeds slated for defence spending. The General Services Administration had put the case that there was no need for the stockpile; at that stage the government held 139.5 million ounces, stored at West Point and in San Francisco. The armed forces required silver for batteries, photographic and x-ray films, dental fillings, surgical plates and electronic components, but if there was to be war it had been decided that sufficient silver could be sourced from Canada and Mexico, as well as from mines within the United States.

Two years earlier President Jimmy Carter had moved to sell off a small amount of the silver (just fifteen million ounces in all) but that was blocked in Congress by the House Armed Services Committee. One congressman, Larry McDonald of Georgia, stated that the government should actually be buying *more* silver. The silver vein in U.S. politics still ran deep; while denying the silver request, the committee approved the sale from the strategic stockpile of 5.5 million carats of industrial diamonds.

But the silver flame in American hearts does not flicker: in 2017, the United States imported twenty-two per cent of the silver sold that year (just over 5,470 tonnes). Yet the country has gone from being the world's top silver producer in 1915 (when it mined forty per cent of the world's silver) to ninth now (and producing four per cent of mine supply).

(In fact, Americans can just look across the Mexican border and there's plenty of silver being mined there. It is not possible to exaggerate how significant Mexico is to silver. The great El Oro mining district was in operation by 1530 and the country was by the eighteenth century the world's greatest producer, overtaking Peru as the main supplier. The Mexican silver dollar, the coins noted for their purity and consistency, were once the used as the means of exchange for foreign trade with Spain, China and Japan — and were in wide circulation in both China and Japan as a currency for domestic business dealings, a role that ended once China started minting its own silver coins and Japan opted for paper money.)

But now the focus is on silver's role as a technology metal — and nothing stands still in this world of technology metals.

One of the most exciting new uses in recent years has been the use of silver in medicine (including dressings and instruments) because of the metal being an antimicrobial agent; that is, it destroys micro-organisms that could carry disease. But in early 2018 the Silver Institute reported on research from a Czech university showing that at least one strain of *Escherichia coli*

(E-coli to you and me) can become resistant to silver nanoparticles after repeated exposure. But the Czechs then came up with a chemical mix that could be used to reverse that. But it is just one more example of how quickly the ground can move under technology stories.

However, there is a more serious challenge facing silver: its use on solar panels.

It was only as recently as January 2016 that Keith Neumeyer of First Majestic Silver Corp in Canada was predicting a silver price of $190/oz by 2019 (compared to $16/oz as it was then). Neumeyer's argument was that the planet was being electrified (electric cars, solar panels) and silver was the most electrically conductive material on the planet apart from gold.

The metal's used in solar panels made it easy to sell (and believe) a bullish story. In 2015 the solar industry had consumed seventy-eight ounces of silver, up twenty-four per cent on the previous year. By 2015 the solar sector accounted for seventeen per cent of all silver used in industrial applications: silver is a primary ingredient in the photovoltaic cells that catch the sun's rays and transform them into energy.

Bullish, too, was analyst Simona Gambarini of Capital Economics who sent out a note in January 2016 expecting silver demand by the solar sector in that year to grow another twenty per cent due to the vast number of solar panels being installed across China. That country's National Energy Administration announced plans to increase solar capacity by twenty gigawatts a year for five years. Gambarini was not concerned about thrifting as an issue: as silver paste accounted for only five per cent of the total cost of photovoltaic panels, there was no great pressure to reduce the amount of silver being used.

Two years on and she had changed her mind. 'We think thrifting and substitution will dent silver demand from the sector and lead to lower prices further ahead,' she wrote in April 2018. Not that there was any slowdown on solar's spread. In 2017 ninety-nine gigawatts of new capacity was added worldwide, thirty per cent more than the previous year, with China accounting for about half that total. And it was expected to keep on growing with the International Energy Agency forecasting world solar growth of seventy gigawatts on average each year for following next decade. The problem, said Gambarini, was the cost of silver, accounting for up to fifteen per cent of a panel's cost (yet its price had not changed much since her 2016 note).

By early 2018 efforts are now under way to reduce the amount of silver being used. 'We estimate that the amount of silver needed to generate one gigawatt of electricity from solar has fallen from 4.98 million ounces in 2006 to 0.93 million ounces in 2017 — an eighty per cent reduction,' she wrote. In fact, research was becoming focused on eliminating entirely the use of silver in solar cells. Natcore Technology of the US had already found a way to replace silver with much cheaper aluminium.

Back on the positive side, demand for silver is also promising regarding radio frequency identification tags, with a forecast six-fold rise in silver use to 367 tonnes a year by 2020. These tags are rapidly taking over from the bar code system. China is now using the technology for ID cards for its populace while European Union passports also include the tags.

In the longer term, the manufacture of wood preservatives could become a significant market for silver. In health care, silver is used as a biocide — an agent capable of destroying organisms — in wound care, catheters, pacemakers, heart valves and feeding tubes. Silver-imbedded equipment may prove the answer to the so far persistent 'superbug', or 'Staph', that is a big worry in hospitals around the world. Bandages often now include silver ions to combat bacteria growth. Ointments are being made with silver as an ingredient, the metal helping with the healing of wounds. By 2020, around 600 tonnes a year of silver could be going into the health market.

Clean water is another big market. Silver is replacing chlorine in filtration (and the metal's use in this regard also eliminates Legionnaire's Disease lurking in pipes and water tanks). Silver as a component of water purification in helping to remove bacteria, chlorine, lead and particulates. Annual consumption of silver in this sector should reach 1,400 tonnes by 2020. Moreover, future use in the developing world could be enormous, given that so many diseases that afflict people there are water-borne.

Silver may be the key to bio-batteries. Stanford University has produced a study that the institute says may help scientists and engineers in their quest for the production of so-called bio-batteries that can produce substantial amounts of electricity from wastewater, contaminants and sewage. They think they can connect bacteria directly to electrodes. The Stanford team found that when silver oxide is introduced to the area around the positive electrode, the silver compound consumes electrons, literally pulling them out of the bacteria and sending them on their way as electricity.

And medicine is seeing increasing applications of the white metal, too. Scientists at the University of Toledo have been working on a problem: silver is being used as a medium to deliver drugs into patients, in cell imaging and other applications. Silver nanoparticles have some drawbacks. The most critical is that the silver readily oxidises allowing it to degrade quickly once inside the body. Instead, gold was used in many applications because it was more stable albeit more expensive. The scientists now think they have the problem licked and have been able to create stable silver nanoparticles. Terry Bigioni, a chemist at the university, says the purity of the new silver ones is a huge advantage for biomedical applications.

Silver can make producing hydrogen more efficient. 'Water splitting', or artificial photosynthesis, is a way to convert the energy of sunlight into chemical energy to produce hydrogen and oxygen. The hydrogen can then be used for clean energy, especially in vehicles. Now, to make that process more efficient, scientists are using a zinc-oxide/silver photo electrode which is very susceptible to sunlight. A laser is directed at a silver oxide film, which loosens silver particles. The silver enhances the light-collecting properties of zinc oxide, meaning much more sunlight is absorbed. The result, according to the research team at the National Taiwan University, results in up to 200 per cent more hydrogen than without the silver particles.

Did you know that adhesive plasters, or sticking plasters, (at least in Europe) sold at pharmacies often contain minute loadings of silver? The metal is known to inhibit bacterial growth, and is being used in all sorts of dressings as well as in catheters and pacemakers. A wide range of leisure wear is made with silver-impregnated textiles, the silver content cutting levels of bacteria that create body odour.

In a back-to-the-future development, photography is doing a vinyl. Just as many music purists prefer those twelve-inch records that rotate on a turntable to the CD, so some photo buffs think the old silver halide film produces richer images than digital. There are still 300 Polaroid cameras in existence around the world, incidentally. And in 2008 a group called The Impossible Project saved the last remaining instant film production plant (in the Netherlands), So silver is still going into film.

On the investment side, in 2011 the Hong Kong Mercantile Exchange began trading a silver futures contract, hoping to tap into the growing demand for the metal in China. Silver demand rose by sixty-seven per cent in China between 2008 and 2010 (against seventeen per cent globally in that period). This should be no surprise: the white metal was the standard for currency from the time of the Ming dynasty until 4 November 1935. It was abandoned then only because, as investors sought safe havens during the Great Depression, the price of silver rose sharply and China could not control the silver price.

If you're looking for silver investment clues anywhere but China, then you're looking in the wrong place. Over the past twenty years, that country has gone from consuming three per cent of the world's silver to sixteen per cent now; but, in parallel, China's share of production over the same time period has gone from five per cent to fourteen per cent, making it both the world's second largest consumer and third largest producer. Since 2007, China has been a net importer of silver.

A few years ago Jim Rogers, former George Soros partner and now an investment guru offering advice from his Singapore base, wrote: 'Buy yourself some silver chopsticks or some silver cutlery — you will be very rich in five or ten years'.

We have seen in India the poorer investors opt for silver because they cannot afford meaningful quantities of gold. It will be something to witness if their Chinese counterparts do the same.

In early 2018 we learned of another problem in the silver industry. With gold the challenge is finding new deposits that can replace what has been mined out. For silver, the struggle is to maintain grades, more critical than with gold because of the great disparity of the price each metal can command.

It's fine if you are mining at more than fifteen ounces a ton. Not so good when the grade is five ounces a tonne or below, and made worse if there is a spike in energy prices. Investors may have been misled, too, if companies still quote the cash cost of producing silver. By contrast, gold mining companies have moved over to what is called all-in sustaining costs (or AISC). The World Gold Council has convinced many companies to use this measure, which includes such things as the capital cost of mine development and administration overheads per ounce of gold mined. Also, the cash cost of silver can be reduced by taking into account by-product receipts, such as any base metals produced.

Silver's big issue now is that, across many of the major mines, grades are falling.

Appendix 3:
Gold Facts

The top gold producing countries (2017, in tonnes — estimated)

China	440
Australia	300
Russia	255
U.S.	245
Canada	180
Peru	155
South Africa	145
Mexico	110
Uzbekistan	100
Indonesia	80
Ghana	80

The top gold miners 2017 (tonnes)

Barrick Gold	165.6
Newmont Mining	163.8
AngloGold Ashanti	111.6

Kinross Gold   81

GoldCorp   79.9

Navoi Mining & Met* 77

Newcrest Mining**   71.1

Polyus Gold***   67.2

Gold Fields   62.6

Agnico Eagle   53.3

* Ukraine ** Australia *** Russia

For the record, here are the annual average prices per ounce of gold:

2001 $273

2002 $310

2003 $363

2004 $409

2005 $444

2006 $604

2007 $695

2008 $872

2009 $973

2010 $1,226

2011 $1,571

2012 $1,668

2013 $1,411

2014 $1,266

2015 $1,257

2016 $1,250

2017 $1,1660

OTHER BOOKS BY ROBIN BROMBY (AND AVAILABLE AT AMAZON IN BOTH E-BOOK AND PAPERBACK FORMAT)

Railways: Their Life & Times. Facts, Figures and Curiosities about Trains from Steam to High Speed

If you were going to try and pick a point when what we think of as "the Great Railway Age" came to an end, then 1965 would be as good as any. Steam was either gone from railway networks, or it was on its last legs: rail travel was no longer the only viable long-distance (land) transport mode; the proliferation of the motor car and the growth in jet passenger aircraft capability offered attractive travel options. More and more railway stations and lines were being closed in parts of the Western world, meaning that no longer would the bulk of people have regular contact with long-distance trains. But the fascination with railways and their history would endure— and this book captures the continuing appeal of trains, looking back over a century to the many stories that need to be told. This is a book for those who love railways.

New Zealand Railways: Their Life & Times

New Zealand railway builders surmounted many obstacles: the terrain, a sparse and scattered population, two islands separated by an often stormy stretch of water, demands from every small settlement for their own railway line. But build a railway system — and a comprehensive one at that — New

Zealand did. This is the story of that railway, from its heyday to the day of reckoning as losses had to be confronted.

By 1953 the pattern was clear. The era of railways as the mainstay of land transport throughout New Zealand was ending. One by one, most of the rural branches would disappear over the next forty years; passenger train travel — other than commuter services in Auckland and Wellington — would almost disappear to a stage where there are just a handful of tourist services on the most scenic lines; all but the largest towns would lose their railway station.

But, until then, the railways of New Zealand were part of almost everyone's life: you caught the train to visit friends and relatives in other parts of New Zealand, you depended on the trains to carry the bulk of the freight that moved to and from the ports. This is their story. Profusely illustrated with photographs and maps. (*E-book and paperback*)

Australian Railways: Their Life and Times

'Picture a small wayside country station. It is unmanned but there is a siding with a few empty four-wheeled wagons; these may have brought bagged fertilizer for local farmers, or they may be left there for a farmer to load bales of wool or bags of wheat. On the platform sit cream cans — full, as it happens — so there must be a train due to collect them and cart them off to the nearest butter factory. Until that train arrives, there will be hardly a sound apart from the wind in the trees behind the station. Then, eventually, we hear the train approaching; it glides to a halt, the cream cans are rolled into the van, the van doors are slammed shut, the locomotive whistle is heard, and the train is on its way again. Within a few minutes, the place is once more silent.'

The nightmare of three different gauges, the daunting challenge of building railways across vast open spaces often with no water supplies, the follies of railway lines that were rarely used—all this is the saga of Australian railways, the sheer hard work and suffering of those who gave their life in service to the railways. Brimming with anecdotes and colorful stories,

Australian Railways: Their Life and Times documents the old, the odd and the now forgotten. Complete with rare historic photographs. (*E-book and paperback*)

Fighting on Empty: How Hitler and Hirohito Lost the Economic War

Nazi Germany, Imperial Japan and Fascist Italy all embarked on their Second World War plans of conquest without one vital factor: sound economies that could absorb and withstand the stresses of total war. In this groundbreaking study, Robin Bromby shows how all three Axis powers went into battle with seriously flawed economies, inadequate industrial capacity and deficient food security. When they invaded much of Europe and East Asia, the Nazis and their partners only compounded the problem: they had made few plans to manage their conquests and failed to harness captured factories and farms.

It was a fatal flaw: their war plans were doomed. Despite the legend of a beleaguered Britain, that country was the largest economy in Europe and was soon building more aircraft than Germany – and had its empire on which to call. Japan's lack of economic planning was breathtaking and the strains soon began to show. And then came the Americans with all their economic power. The Axis was finished.

Fighting on Empty reveals a largely ignored, but crucial, aspect of the Second World War. (*E-book and paperback*)

German Raiders of the South Seas: The extraordinary true story of naval deception, daring and disguise 1914-1917.

Far from the mud and slaughter of the Western Front, there was another face of the Great War — an oddly stirring and thrilling one, characterized by chivalry and remarkably few casualties. This is the story of how three German naval surface raiders disrupted British shipping across large swathes of the Indian and Pacific oceans between 1914 and 1917. Attempts to supply critical cargoes and much needed reinforcements for the trenches in France and Belgium were hamstrung by German daring on the high seas.

Were it not all real and true, it would make wonderful fiction: the buccaneering crew of the *Emden* casting a shadow of fear over an ocean; the survivors of the battle with the Sydney sailing a leaking copra schooner from the Cocos Islands to the East Indies; the *Wolf* steaming undetected around the coasts of Australia and New Zealand laying mines that later would claim merchant shipping, then capturing a passenger vessel and sailing it to the East Indies; victims the captain of the *Seeadler*, von Luckner, sailing a small boat halfway across the Pacific to Fiji, and then later making a dramatic escape from a New Zealand prisoner of war camp.

In the first days of World War I a German light cruiser detached itself from the East Asiatic Squadron with the mission to raid and harass Allied shipping. The ship, SMS Emden, not only became world famous in its two months of raiding, during which it sank sixteen ships and captured others, but demonstrated the vulnerability of Australian, New Zealand and Empire shipping links. (*e-book and paperback*)

The Farming of Australia: A saga of backbreaking toil and tenacity

This is the story of triumph over a dry, hot and often infertile land. Australia's farmers have overcome difficult terrain and the tyranny of distance to make the country an important food bowl. This is the story of 200-plus years of ups and downs from savage droughts and daunting challenges to the triumphs of irrigation and imagination and inventiveness. (*E-book and paperback*)

Newspapers: A Century of Failure. Why the Internet was the Last Straw that Broke the Industry

From the broadcast of the first news bulletin on radio in 1920, daily newspapers have been under pressure from a succession of challenges, ranging from television to suburban weeklies until—finally—the internet delivered its near-fatal blow. Along the way since 1920, the industry has been beset by industrial disputes, reluctance to embrace the latest technologies, crippling rises in costs of newsprint and labour, traffic gridlock that hampered city newspaper deliveries. By the time it became possible to get your news on a computer, and then on other mobile devices, the newspaper industry was passed its best. Then many papers made the near fatal decision to give away their news for free online, a strategy that was realised too late to be a dreadful mistake. *Newspapers: A Century of Decline* charts this century-long saga. (*paperback and e-book*)

Go to www.highgatepublishing.com.au for further details and free extracts.

www.ingramcontent.com/pod-product-compliance
Lightning Source LLC
Chambersburg PA
CBHW032011190326
41520CB00007B/429